ACUPUNCTURE AND ORIENTAL MEDICINE
STATE LAWS AND REGULATIONS

2005 EDITION

ACUPUNCTURE AND ORIENTAL MEDICINE
STATE LAWS AND REGULATIONS

2005 EDITION

NAF
PUBLICATIONS

Gig Harbor, Washington

National Acupuncture Foundation
6405 43rd Avenue Ct NW, Ste B
Gig Harbor, WA 98335
(253) 851-6538
www.nationalacupuncturefoundation.org
Copyright 2005 National Acupuncture Foundation
All rights reserved, including the right to reproduce this work in any form whatsoever, without permission in writing from the publisher, except for brief passages in connection with a review.
Printed in the USA

ISBN: 0-9670262-9-6

Library of Congress Control Number: 2004115444

Cover and book design by Tierney Tully

If you are unable to order this book from your local bookseller, please call us.
Quantity discounts for schools and organizations are available.

Notice: The information in this book is true and complete to the best of our knowledge. It is offered without guarantee on the part of the editor or the National Acupuncture Foundation. The editor and National Acupuncture Foundation disclaim all liability in connection with the use of this book.

CONTENTS

Tables

Resources

FOREWORD

by Michael H. Cohen, J.D.

For several years, Barbara Mitchell's *Acupuncture and Oriental Medicine State Laws* has been an indispensable resource for practitioners, attorneys, and regulators, both in acupuncture and Oriental medicine, and in the field of complementary and alternative medicine (CAM) more generally. Barbara Mitchell, JD, L.Ac., is to be commended for her early and insightful compilations of relevant statutes, regulations, and other regulatory material, including model provisions. This new edition continues to build on that wonderful foundation.

The book's thorough research makes it easy to trace relevant legal authority, and as well, to follow through with appropriate officials and locate up-to-date information. The research is comprehensive, detailed, and on-point. Notably, Barbara Mitchell's earlier work, now brought current with the latest developments, highlights the body of regulation that can be critical to understanding such issues as licensure and scope of practice, credentialing, insurance, and professional practice.

The practice of acupuncture and Oriental medicine has emerged over several decades as a respected healing profession alongside an array of others making important contributions to patient health. From humble origins in the 1970's as an import from the East and, in the eyes of skeptics, maverick sideline to conventional care, the profession has grown in stature and significance. Practitioners of acupuncture and Oriental medicine now work not only independently and in association with other CAM providers across the country, but also in surgical wards, pain centers, intensive care units, and elsewhere within conventional medical settings.

More broadly, U.S. health care is moving past a parochial focus on biomedicine toward inclusion of a larger spectrum of healing traditions and modalities, including not only acupuncture and Oriental medicine, but also naturopathic medicine, massage therapy, and chiropractic. Once marginalized and dismissed, these disciplines now have established programs for professional training; professional bodies for accreditation of schools; mechanisms to establish professional consensus on ethical codes and standards for professional practice, and road maps to licensure in some, most, or in the case of chiropractic, all, states.

The notion of "integrative care"—initially popularized by Andrew Weil, M.D.—brought into mainstream language by a variety of articles published in peer-reviewed medical literature, and adopted by the National Center for Complementary and Alternative Medicine (NCCAM) at the National Institutes of Health-resonates with wider efforts to integrate such therapies with biomedical care. "Integration" also suggests the acceptance of complementary and alternative medical providers as peers alongside medical doctors-cross-referring, sharing diagnostic and treatment plans, and otherwise collaborating in the best interest of the patient. Such integration is occurring on many levels, whether within an integrative care clinic designated as such inside an academically affiliated hospital; an association of providers outside a hospital system; or a referral network among and between a diversity of providers, whether styled as "conventional" or "CAM."

Beyond the clinical setting, the research community is intensely active in examination of integration's potential contours. The theory and practice of acupuncture and Oriental medicine is neither completely accepted nor completely understood by researchers; yet, as scientific investigation continues delving into safety, efficacy, and mechanism, philosophical bridges are being built, augmenting interpretive conversations across cultures.

Within this new care environment, it becomes increasingly important not only for CAM providers and their professional regulatory boards, but also biomedical professionals (and regulators), to familiarize themselves with laws and regulations relevant to acupuncture and Oriental medicine. For example, physicians, whose patients request referrals to acupuncture and Oriental medicine practitioners, may wish to understand the basics of such providers' licensure; similarly, those involved in credentialing acupuncture and Oriental medicine practitioners would want to understand the regulatory and professional framework that serves as legal

FOREWORD

scaffolding for the profession. Moreover, understanding such regulatory issues as scope of practice varia-tions across states may help clinical researchers learn how better to design trials testing individual thera-peutic modalities.

In short, integration has professional practice as well as clinical research, legal and regulatory, and one might add, ethical dimensions. In a larger sense, knowing and understanding the regulatory structure, as well as theories and modalities, pertinent to acupuncture and Oriental medicine can help facilitate a true cross-pol-lination of approaches to clinical care across disciplines. In this light, the present edition of *Acupuncture and Oriental Medicine State Laws and Regulations* can become a critical reference for those in different health-care fields. The book no doubt will serve as a catalyst for deeper conversation among healing professionals of all walks and propensities, as well as the regulators who serve them and the public.

Michael H. Cohen, J.D.
Cambridge, Massachusetts
www.camlawblog.com

ABOUT THIS BOOK

This book provides an overview of the regulation of acupuncture practice in the United States. The information presented in the individual state listings, in most cases, has been summarized. However, no attempt has been made to interpret laws or regulations. If information in the state listings seems incomplete or is not clear, the reader is directed to the appropriate state regulatory agency for clarification.

Regulatory agencies in all fifty states were contacted and asked to contribute the latest information possible about the regulation of acupuncture within their state. Effort was focused on those agencies in those states that have passed acupuncture legislation and which are directly involved in regulation of "professional acupuncturists." For the purposes of this book, "professional acupuncturist" is defined as a healthcare practitioner whose primary practice and licensure is in the profession of acupuncture, or acupuncture and Oriental medicine. Medical and chiropractic boards were also contacted for information about the practice of acupuncture by their licensees and that information has been reported where available, including information on the practice of acupuncture by podiatrists, dentists, physician assistants, naturopaths, and others if provided.

If the responses received from the agencies appeared to be well considered and thorough, any changes to previous information were made based on the agency's response. In the case of those agencies not responding (2), or if the response did not appear to be complete, every effort was made to update information from public documents available. Even in the event that all information was correct at the time of acquisition (late 2004 for this edition), the regulatory process is a fluid one and changes are ongoing. There is no guarantee that the information contained in this book will be correct at the time the reader encounters it. In any case, where the information is to be used in matters that require utmost accuracy, the reader is advised to contact the state regulatory agency directly for the most current and accurate information.

This is the seventh edition of this publication. The format of the book will appear familiar to those who have copies of previous editions. However, efforts have been made to make the presentation of the material easier to read and access, and to standardize terminology, abbreviations, spelling, etc. where possible. Changes in statute or regulation have been noted in each state listing and/or in the tables at the end of the book. The introductory chapter on regulation is entirely new and we present it to assist the reader unfamiliar with the regulatory process understand some of the common issues surrounding the regulation of acupuncture.

I would like to make the following acknowledgements of those who contributed to this book.

First of all, this project would not have been possible if not for the work done by Barbara Mitchell on the six previous editions of this book. My thanks to Barbara for her attention to detail and documentation, which allowed me to pick up where she left off.

I wish to thank the individuals at the regulatory agencies who understood the value of this project and graciously gave of their time to provide the information needed. Their assistance has been invaluable. There were many contributors to the book and each of them need to be thanked for their interest and assistance.

- ❖ The Council of Colleges of Acupuncture and Oriental Medicine (CCAOM) for permission to reprint their one-page guide, "Know Your Acupuncturist;"

- ❖ Michael H. Cohen, J.D., Director of Legal Programs for the Harvard Medical School Division for Research and Education in Complementary and Integrative Therapies and Harvard Medical School Osher Institute, who wrote the Foreword to the book and reviewed the chapter on regulation;

- ❖ Penny Heisler, Executive Director of the Maryland Board of Acupuncture and Treasurer and Public Relations Chair for the Federation of Acupuncture and Oriental Medicine Regulatory Agencies

ABOUT THIS BOOK

(FAOMRA) for information on FAOMRA's efforts to establish licensure endorsement between states.

❖ Debra Howard, L.M.T., Dipl.ABT (NCCAOM), President of the American Organization of Bodywork Therapies of Asia (AODTA) for providing information on the credentialing of Asian bodywork therapists;

❖ Rachel Toomim, A.P., board member of the National Acupuncture Detoxification Association (NADA) for providing the information on acupuncture detoxification;

❖ Betsy Smith, Director of Applicant and State Relations at the National Certification Commission for Acupuncture and Oriental Medicine (NCCAOM) for information regarding NCCAOM's certification programs.

❖ Mark Christensen, Ph.D., Assistant Executive Director and Director of Testing at the National Board of Chiropractic Examiners (NBCE) for information on the board's acupuncture certification process for chiropractors;

❖ Sherman Cohn, J.D., Professor of Law at Georgetown University Law School and president of the National Acupuncture Foundation, for his significant contribution to the chapter on regulation, for providing assistance with the organization of the book and reviewing the manuscript, and for providing me with tremendous support in the undertaking of this project.

The NAF plans to continue expanding the scope of this book in future editions. We welcome your comments and suggestions about how to improve it and make it more useful.

Tierney Tully, M.S.O.M., Dipl.Ac. (NCCAOM)
Executive Director
National Acupuncture Foundation

ABBREVIATIONS

ACAOM - Accreditation Commission for Acupuncture and Oriental Medicine
        Formerly known as: National Accreditation Commission for Schools and Colleges
        of Acupuncture and Oriental Medicine (NACSCAOM)

ADS - Acupuncture Detoxification Specialist

AOBTA - Association of Body Work Therapies of Asia

CCAOM - Council of Colleges of Acupuncture and Oriental Medicine

CCE - Council on Chiropractic Education

CDR - Credentials Documentation Review

CE - Continuing Education

CEU - Continuing Education Unit

CNT - Clean Needle Technique

CPR- Cardio-Pulmonary Resuscitation

CSE - Clinical Skills Examination

D.O. - Doctor of Osteopathy

D.C. - Doctor of Chiropractic

D.P.M. - Doctor of Podiatric Medicine

D.D.S. - Doctor of Dental Surgery

FDA - Food and Drug Administration

L.Ac. - Licensed Acupuncturist

NCCAOM - National Certification Commission of Acupuncture and Oriental Medicine

NIH - National Institutes for Health

NADA - National Acupuncture Detoxification Association

OSHA - Occupational Safety and Health Administration

P.A. - Physician Assistant

P.T. - Physical Therapist

PEPLS - Practical Examination of Point Location Skills (NCCAOM)

TOEFL - Test of English as a Foreign Language

TSE - Test of Spoken English

THE REGULATION OF ACUPUNCTURE IN THE UNITED STATES

Background

Why is there no national licensing for acupuncturists? Why are the requirements for licensure so different from state to state? Why is it that an acupuncturist licensed and practicing in Maryland for thirty years can't get a license in New Mexico? Why can medical doctors and often dentists and chiropractors practice acupuncture with no training?

As with much in the United States, the answer lies in history and in law. And, the answer is not as clear and black and white as one would desire. Generally, professional regulation is a state issue, not a federal one.

It is arguable that Congress could directly regulate the licensing of professions as a aspect of its power over commerce. It is also arguable that, under the Tenth Amendment to the United States Constitution, regulation of a profession is a local matter reserved to the individual States. Whatever the power of Congress, so far it has not attempted to regulate the professions directly. Thus, licensing and scope of practice of the professions, as well as the discipline of professionals, has been left to the states.

The terms "generally" and "directly" of course imply that there are some exceptions. Clearly, Congress has the power to, and has regulated pharmaceuticals and non-pharmaceutical "supplements" that are shipped from state to state or imported. The federal government also has the power to regulate medical devices, including acupuncture needles and electroacupuncture devices, that are imported or shipped from state to state. And through its power to "recognize" private agencies that accredit schools and colleges, the federal government has the power to put certain restrictions and requirements upon schools and colleges that educate and train acupuncturists. For a student to qualify for a government-guaranteed student loan, he or she must attend a school or college accredited by an agency which is recognized by the United States Department of Education—thus giving the Department, acting under the Higher Education Act, significant power over the educational requirements of all professions.

With those exceptions, however, the power to license and regulate each profession lies in the states and will continue to be in the states unless or until the federal government decides to intrude even further and even then, federal regulation will need to pass constitutional muster. Thus, unless a state violates the federal restrictions on discrimination or the federal requirements of due process, each state has the power to determine the qualifications for licensure, the scope of practice permitted a person who is licensed, and the disciplining of a licensee who is charged with violating the scope of practice or other requirement of the state.

Various modalities of healthcare were accepted practices in the United States until the end of the 19th and the early 20th century—folk medicine, botanical healing, homeopathy, midwifery, "eclectic" medicine. While there was some regulation of medical practice going back into the 18th Century, it was sporadic and weakly enforced. However, beginning after the Civil War, practitioners of what would come to be called allopathic medicine gained control of the licensing apparatus in state after state. These practitioners appreciated the power of the law and controlled the medical board in each state. Through the regulatory boards, allopathic practitioners then set standards for the education required to qualify for a license to practice medicine—including requiring graduation from an allopathic medical school, which ultimately put out of business all those schools teaching other healing arts. The regulatory statutes passed on the state level and the medical boards also defined the scope of practice for an allopathic medical doctor quite broadly.

These developments had several effects. First, whatever was recognized as within a medical doctor's scope of practice could be practiced without any specific training on that particular subject or technique. Second, anyone else who practiced that modality—or any other modality and claimed to be practicing a healing art —was subject to being accused as practicing medicine without a license, which is a crime. And, third, should a medical doctor go outside the scope of practice as defined by the medical board, he or she could be accused of "unprofessional conduct" and be subject to discipline, including loss of licensure. In this way, allopathic medicine protected its own turf against others practicing medicine and, at the same time, restricted physicians to what was conventionally acceptable. The combination of these factors meant that, a licensed physician could not practice homeopathy or other modalities rejected by allopathic medicine without being subject to charge of unprofessional conduct. And a non-physician who attempted to heal with such modalities would be charged with practicing medicine without a license.

Central to this situation is that the medical boards and the medical societies have been well organized and vigilant, seeking intervention and disciplinary action whenever a non-physician practiced a healing art or a physician engaged in "unprofessional conduct." But they could not do it alone. Having the distinction of being the dominant and accepted authority in all things healthcare related, the medical community found support from the established prosecutorial authorities, who in the final analysis must bring and prosecute any charges.

The first alternative practitioners to successfully challenge this state-sanctioned monopoly were the chiropractors. They were the first to succeed in obtaining legal recognition as a profession distinct from conventional medicine. Their efforts, of course, were not welcomed by the medical community. Throughout the first three quarters of the 20th Century, the medical societies and medical regulatory bodies and the chiropractic community waged bitter battles. But, starting in 1921 with Georgia, state after state passed laws providing for the licensing of chiropractors and defining the practice of chiropractic. By 1974, each of the fifty states had such a law.

Conventional medicine, however, tried to limit the success of chiropractic as much as possible. Physicians, for example, who referred patients for chiropractic therapy, or lectured at a chiropractic college, or in any other way associated with a chiropractor, were guilty of unprofessional conduct and subject to discipline. Thus, chiropractors could not be admitted to practice in hospitals; nor could an allopathic physician join in a clinic with a chiropractor. In 1976, four chiropractors, with the support of the chiropractic profession, filed a lawsuit against the American Medical Association for attempting to monopolize the health-care delivery system in violation of the federal antitrust laws. It took eight years of litigation, but in 1984, the AMA was found guilty of conducting an illegal boycott in restraint of trade. The practices of allopathic medicine to limit the success of chiropractors ended.

Since the mid-1970s, of course, statutes have also been passed providing for the licensing of acupuncturists, of naturopaths, and of massage therapists. However, these professions are dealt with as exceptions to conventional, allopathic medicine. As exceptions, the statutory scope of practice of the alternatives to allopathic medicine is narrowly defined.

Regulation of Acupuncture

The first statutes authorizing the licensing or registration of professional acupuncturists (individuals whose primary practice and licensure is in acupuncture) were enacted in the early 1970's. Today forty states and the District of Columbia have enacted such statutes. In addition, Michigan and Kansas allow non-physician acupuncturists to practice under the supervision of a licensed medical doctor. In the remaining eight states, acupuncture is either unregulated and no determination has been made regarding the practice of acupuncture, or it has been determined to be the practice of medicine.

The legislative process is often long and difficult. In most states, it took several years to persuade a legislature to pass, and a governor to sign, an acupuncture practice act. Moreover, as there is usually significant opposition from established healthcare professionals, compromises are often necessary. Even in some of the states that have passed acupuncture practice acts, the statute requires supervision, referral, or prior diagnosis by a medical doctor before a patient may receive acupuncture treatment from a licensed acupuncturist. However, the trend is toward more independence for professional acupuncturists. The supervision and/or referral requirement was removed in Illinois and the District of Columbia in 2004, and the requirement in Pennsylvania changed from supervision to referral with prior diagnosis in 2002. Only twelve states that regulate acupuncture now require some form of sanction by the conventional medical community before a professional acupuncturist may treat a patient.

In all professional practice statutes, a regulatory agency is either created or designated to oversee the profession. The type of agency differs state by state. Thirteen states have independent acupuncture boards, twenty-seven states and the District of Columbia are governed under other agencies such as the Department of Health or the Board of Medicine. Sixteen of those twenty-seven states have acupuncture advisory committees that make recommendations to the regulatory body on matters related to acupuncture practice.

Acupuncture practice statutes and regulations vary tremendously from state to state. In most states, the statute defines what acupuncture, or acupuncture practice, is and sometimes defines eligibility requirements for licensure. In others, the regulatory board is charged with defining scope of practice and licensure eligibility. The rules and regulations in some states are very detailed about the scope of practice and precisely how many hours and of what type of training are needed to be eligible for licensure. Some list extensive procedures for conducting board business, for disciplinary actions, and other matters. State regulatory boards have broad authority to interpret and elaborate as long as the rules and regulations do not contradict the provisions of the statute nor constitutional due process requirements.

Some state laws and rules governing the practice of acupuncture are simple, straightforward, and easy to understand. Others are complex and difficult. In some states, neither statute nor rule clarifies the scope of practice and there are allowances for interpretation. For instance, the term "acupuncture," may be interpreted as only the insertion of needles, or it may infer the whole of Oriental medicine theory and practice, including the use of Oriental herbs, Oriental massage, dietary advice, therapeutic exercises, etc. In such cases, interpretation occurs on a case-by-case basis, sometimes by the regulatory board, sometimes by legal decision. When regulation is left up to such interpretation, it may be changed quite easily by a new interpretation in a subsequent case or by a change in appointed administrative officials.

The reason for such differences between states is due to a variety of factors. Primarily, passage of a professional practice act is a political process. Legislation must be sponsored by one or more legislators and the language in the bill must be agreeable to interested parties that may have a stake in its passage or defeat. In some cases, such interested parties may have considerable political "clout" and be able to significantly influence the outcome of a profession's legislative effort. Sometimes, troubled legislation can be saved if opposing groups can agree on acceptable language.

Setting Professional Standards for Acupuncture Practice

The acupuncture profession has made admirable progress with developing professional standards. In the early 1980's the acupuncture professional community founded national organizations for the purpose of standardizing educational programs for acupuncture and for certifying practitioners in competency. Among the organizations established was the Accreditation Commission for Acupuncture and Oriental Medicine (ACAOM). ACAOM, upon consultation with schools and colleges of acupuncture, acupuncture professional associations, and other members of the acupuncture community, created standards for education and clinical training for master's level degree programs in acupuncture, and in acupuncture and Oriental medicine. The standards have undergone evolution over the past twenty plus years. Currently, the masters level standard for acupuncture programs is three years in length requiring at least 1,905 hours of didactic and clinical training. The master's level standard for acupuncture and Oriental medicine programs is four years in length requiring at least 2,625 hours of didactic and clinical training, including curricula in Chinese herbal medicine. More recently, ACAOM developed standards for postgraduate doctoral programs for those who wish to pursue their education beyond the master's level. Currently, four educational institutions—Bastyr University in Seattle, Washington, Oregon College of Oriental Medicine in Portland, Oregon, Emperor's College in Los

THE REGULATION OF ACUPUNCTURE

Angeles, California, and Pacific College of Oriental Medicine in San Diego, California—offer a postgraduate doctorate based on ACAOM standards. The first individuals to earn a doctorate in acupuncture and Oriental medicine from an ACAOM-approved program are scheduled to graduate this year in July from Bastyr University.

ACAOM is the only accrediting agency for acupuncture and Oriental medicine academic programs recognized by the U.S. Department of Education. ACAOM's master's level standards have been adopted by many state regulatory agencies in determining eligibility requirements for licensure. No state, at this time, requires doctoral level education for licensure. A few states, however, have promulgated their own educational standards, some of which exceed ACAOM's master's level standards.

It should be noted that a state licensure title is not the same as a academic degree title. With the exception of the aforementioned new doctoral students, those who are earning degrees in schools and colleges of acupuncture and Oriental medicine at this time are earning master's level degrees, with credentials such as a Master of Acupuncture and Oriental Medicine (M.S.A.O.M.) or Master of Oriental Medicine (M.S.O.M.). In most states, practice statutes define "acupuncture" and the licensure title is "acupuncturist," "registered acupuncturist," certified acupuncturist," "licensed acupuncturist," or "acupuncture physician." In only three states does the title of licensure designate Oriental medicine rather than acupuncture as the practice being licensed. And, in those cases, the title also includes the designation "doctor," as in "doctor of Oriental medicine." However, the title is not reflective of a licensure requirement for doctoral level education and training, nor have the majority of practitioners licensed in those states earned doctorate degrees in acupuncture and/or Oriental medicine.

Also created in the early 1980's was the National Certification Commission for Acupuncture and Oriental Medicine (NCCAOM). The NCCAOM administers national competency examinations in acupuncture, Chinese herbology, and in Asian Bodywork Therapy. NCCAOM now also offers a certification in Oriental Medicine which requires successful completion of examinations in acupuncture, Chinese herbology, and western biosciences. Many states require the NCCAOM exam or certification in acupuncture for licensure, and a few states that include herbal medicine in the scope of practice have required the NCCAOM certification in Chinese herbology as well. No state has yet made the Oriental Medicine certification a mandatory requirement for licensure, although New Mexico has recently revised its examination requirements to include the additional NCCAOM examinations necessary for the Oriental Medicine certification.

Another national organization, the Council of Colleges of Acupuncture and Oriental Medicine (CCAOM), is a membership organization of schools and colleges that offer acupuncture and Oriental medicine degree programs. The Council also administers a clean needle technique course and exam, required by the NCCAOM for certification in acupuncture. It has recently produced a one-page document, *Know Your Acupuncturist*, that describes typical educational levels for various healthcare practitioners who practice acupuncture. It is reprinted here, on the following page, with CCAOM's permission.

These organizations, and other organizations and individuals in the profession, have assisted in creating national entry-level standards for the practice of acupuncture and Oriental medicine. The purpose of establishing national standards was to create an environment that assured state regulators and the public of the competency of professional acupuncturists. It was also hoped that state regulatory agencies would adopt uniform licensure requirements based on national standards which would allow professional acupuncturists to move freely from state to state, thereby facilitating the growth of the profession. Unfortunately, these national standards have not been adopted uniformly, primarily, as mentioned before, due to the political nature of professional regulation. Necessary compromises with other healthcare professional communities have been noted. In addition, in spite of established standards, regulatory efforts have not always been cooperative between individuals and state and national organizations within the acupuncture profession.

Know Your Acupuncturist

Practitioners whose educational focus is in Acupuncture and Oriental Medicine receive approximately 80% of their training exclusively in this field, and undergo an extensive clinical internship averaging 3 years. Other healthcare practitioners may use acupuncture, which is one of the many therapies of Oriental Medicine, as an adjunct to their primary practice. While all of these practitioners also have training in western medical sciences, this chart is designed to illustrate the varying levels of acupuncture training generally undertaken by healthcare professionals.

Amount of Training In Acupuncture	Practitioner
1363 hours to 2000 hours in Acupuncture (or 2000-3000 hours in Oriental Medicine)* *Licensed Acupuncturist* *Traditional Chinese Medicine* *Comprehensively-trained Acupuncturist* *Oriental Medicine Practitioner* *Oriental Medical Acupuncture*	**Typically a Licensed Acupuncturist (L.Ac.)** or Registered Acupuncturist whose primary training is in Acupuncture and/or Oriental Medicine, and has: (a) obtained a 3 to 4-year master's level degree or diploma from a school approved by ACAOM (Accreditation Commission for Acupuncture and Oriental Medicine), and (b) is awarded the Dipl.Ac. (Diplomate in Acupuncture) designation upon successful examination by the NCCAOM (National Commission for the Certification of Acupuncture and Oriental Medicine) which is the national standard used for licensing in most states.** -Used for a broad range of health issues, including chronic disease, pain, internal medicine, rehabilitation, and prevention based on Oriental medical theory.
300 hours or less *Medical Acupuncture* *Meridian Balancing/Therapy* *Chiropractic Acupuncture* *Naturopathic Acupuncture*	**Typically a medical doctor, osteopath, naturopath, or chiropractor** who uses acupuncture as an adjunctive therapy; the World Health Organization (WHO) recommends that medical doctors have 200 hours of training to know when to refer to a more fully-trained Acupuncturist or Oriental Medicine practitioner.*** -Most commonly used for pain and basic ailments.
Around 100 hours or less *Detox Tech* *Chiropractic Acupuncture* *Medical Acupuncture*	**Typically a detoxification technician or chiropractor** (detox techs should be under supervision of a Licensed Acupuncturist, see above, and are limited to 5 points on the ear) -Most commonly used for pain management or addiction & detoxification through auricular acupuncture.

For a list of approved schools and colleges, contact the U.S. Department of Education or:

www.ccaom.org   www.nccaom.org   www.acaom.org

*Many Acupuncture and Oriental Medical schools exceed 2000 hours.

**Acupuncture/Oriental Medical practitioners are able to obtain a D.A.O.M. degree from an ACAOM-approved clinical doctoral program. Some states also designate the licensing title (non degree) as D.O.M. or D.Ac., or Acupuncture Physician. Licensed Acupuncturists may have also obtained an O.M.D., Ph.D., or D.Ac. for non-extensive post-graduate training (from unaccredited programs). Thus, it is important to ask where such a title was received.

***Some medical doctors and chiropractors are trained and licensed in both western and Oriental medical acupuncture. Ask your physician about his or her credentials. Acupuncture should only be administered by a practitioner who has specific training in this field, due to risk of improper needling, inadequate understanding of Oriental medical diagnostic procedures, transmission of disease, imbalancing of energy, or ethical violations.

Produced by the Council of Colleges of Acupuncture and Oriental Medicine (CCAOM). For reprint information contact 301-313-0870. For information about the Council please see our web site at: http://www.ccaom.org

THE REGULATION OF ACUPUNCTURE

Reciprocity and Endorsement

One of the results of such variety in professional regulation is the difficulty practitioners have of moving from state to state. An acupuncture professional, licensed in one state, may easily find that additional educational requirements may need to be fulfilled, as well as additional examination, when he or she applies for licensure in another state. Although this problem is not peculiar to the acupuncture profession, it is a particular problem in a profession, like acupuncture, where the educational standards have evolved significantly in the past quarter century. Thus, an acupuncture professional may find that, after several years of education and internship, and perhaps a decade or two of competent practice, he or she is not eligible to be licensed in a state to which he or she chooses to relocate.

There is virtually no reciprocity between states for acupuncture licensure. Reciprocity requires that, on the basis of licensure of a practitioner in state A, he or she would be granted licensure in state B, but only if state B also allowed licensure of state A's applicants. Currently, no states have entered into such reciprocal agreements.

A different form of waiver is endorsement. Endorsement allows that if the applicant has met requirements in state A that are equivalent to, or exceed, the requirements of state B, that licensure may be granted in state B on that basis. However, only twelve states that license acupuncturists currently have an endorsement provision, and considering that none of them have equivalent licensure requirements, this route of eligibility is largely ineffective as an answer to interstate mobility.

The inequity in current licensing procedures across the country has been taken up by the Federation of Acupuncture and Oriental Medicine Regulatory Agencies (FAOMRA). FAOMRA was established in 1997 to fill a void at the national level for representation of state regulatory issues by boards and agencies regulating the acupuncture and Oriental medicine profession. FAORMA's membership currently includes fourteen states in the United States. The mission of FAOMRA is "to provide an organization through which member agencies may work together to better assure the protection of the public through good communication about licensure, practice, regulatory activity and professional disciplinary action and to promote the delivery of quality healthcare to the public."

To address the need for national licensing standards, FAOMRA is working with other national organizations to identify and develop levels of credentialing and competency standards for licensees of acupuncture and Oriental medicine and to ensure that these standards remain diverse and embrace all traditions of acupuncture and Oriental medicine. The Federation is constructing language to launch licensure by endorsement standards that will facilitate movement of licensees from state to state. The framework for this discussion can be found on FAOMRA's web site at www.faomra.com.

Acupuncture and Other Healthcare Providers

As has been noted, since the mid-1800's, when the medical profession in the United States organized and instituted the regulation of medical practice, the medical profession has dominated the politics of healthcare. Acupuncture is within the scope of practice of licensed medical doctors and osteopaths in forty-nine states and the District of Columbia. Only Hawaii requires an allopathic physician to comply with the requirements of the professional acupuncture licensing act in order to practice acupuncture. Only twelve states specify that a medical doctor have education and training in acupuncture before he or she practices acupuncture. In nine of those states, a specific number of hours of training, ranging from 200-300, are indicated. Louisiana specifies six months of training, and four states simply indicate that training should be "adequate," "appropriate," or "sufficient." In none of these states is a specific training curriculum indicated. In addition, several states allow other conventional healthcare professionals, such as podiatrists, dentists, physician assistants, nurses, and others, to provide acupuncture services within their scope of practice without specific acupuncture training.

THE REGULATION OF ACUPUNCTURE

An obvious concern over this lack of standards would be public safety. However, thirty years of acupuncture use in this country has demonstrated that acupuncture is the safest of medical procedures. Thus, it may be argued that safety is not the primary concern. However, efficacy and competency are different matters.

One difficult concept in the evaluation of the training of those practicing acupuncture is understanding the paradigm in which acupuncture is practiced. If a medical professional uses acupuncture as an additional tool within a western medicine scope of practice, it could be argued that extensive education in Oriental medicine theory and practice is unnecessary; that less than the full range of education and training required of a professional acupuncturist is necessary. If, however, the medical professional identifies himself or herself and his or her primary practice as that of acupuncture, or Oriental medicine, the need for comprehensive education and training in acupuncture and Oriental medicine would appear to be obvious.

One of the concerns of the acupuncture professional community is that, even when training is specified for other health professionals using acupuncture within their scopes, the training is typically described only in numbers of hours with no definition of content or indication of what level of practice is allowed.

The World Health Organization (WHO) Guidelines on Basic Training and Safety in Acupuncture, which are typically employed by medical doctors and chiropractors in those states that require acupuncture training for their licensees, describe four levels of training directly related to the level of practice. They are as follows:

Category of Personnel	Level of training	Acupuncture curriculum	Western biosciences
Non-medical acupuncture practitioners	Full course of training	1000 hours theory 500 hours clinical 500 hours supervised practice	500 hours
Qualified Physicians	Full course of training	500 hours theory 500 hours clinical 500 hours supervised practice	
Qualified Physicians	Limited training for use as a technique in clinical work	Not less than 200 hours	
Other health personnel	Limited training for use in primary healthcare	Varies according to application envisaged	

It is apparent that WHO recognizes that curriculum and length of training is directly tied to the application of acupuncture practice intended by the health professional. It clearly states that a medical doctor who wishes to practice the full scope of acupuncture and Oriental medicine undergo nearly as much training in acupuncture (1,500 hours) as a non-medical acupuncture practitioner (2,000 hours). It also makes clear that the training of other healthcare professionals, who are not medical doctors, should be dependent on the level of practice intended. One would assume that this training would not be less than that required for medical doctors for the level of practice intended.

THE REGULATION OF ACUPUNCTURE

Unfortunately, in the course of acupuncture's thirty-year history in this country, the acupuncture profession has not effectively engaged other healthcare professionals in discussion of what, short of doing a full degree program in acupuncture and Oriental medicine, would constitute adequate training to be able to perform limited acupuncture services within the scope of their primary profession. Moreover, established healthcare professionals that have influence in defining their scope of practice, have found it largely unnecessary to engage in such a dialogue, resulting in most setting no standards for the practice of acupuncture. However, the lack is not complete.

Medical Doctors and Osteopaths

The American Board of Medical Specialties (Established 1933) does not recognize acupuncture as a medical specialty. However, a group of medical doctors interested in acupuncture founded the American Academy of Medical Acupuncture (AAMA) in 1987 in recognition of the interest some of their colleagues were taking in acupuncture and with a desire to set a standard of education for those who wished to practice acupuncture. The AAMA conducts research and educational seminars and provides its members with access to information and materials on the use of acupuncture in western medical environments.

The AAMA defines "medical acupuncture" as follows: "medical acupuncture is a medical discipline having a central core of knowledge embracing the integration of acupuncture from various traditions into contemporary biomedical practice. A Physician Acupuncturist is one who has acquired specialized knowledge and experience related to the integration of acupuncture within a biomedicine practice."

To become a "Fellow" of the Academy, a licensed medical doctor or doctor of osteopathy must have completed at least 200 hours of graduate training in medical acupuncture in a certified program or some equivalent. This standard is based on the previously mentioned WHO criteria for practice of acupuncture by healthcare professionals and on recommendations of the World Federation of Acupuncture and Moxibustion Societies. The AAMA recognizes NCCAOM certification as equivalent to this standard. This acknowledgement is significant, in that, the NCCAOM has no separate or abbreviated certification in acupuncture for non-professional acupuncturists and the training required to earn the NCCAOM diplomate in acupuncture is not based in the western medical paradigm.

To administer its program in certification for medical acupuncture, the American Board of Medical Acupuncture was formally established in 2000 as an independent agency within the AAMA. The board provides a list of approved training programs and administers its certification exam at least once per year. Upon an individual's successful fulfillment of the educational and examination requirements for certification, the board will grant a certificate of board approval as a diplomate of the American Board of Medical Acupuncture (DABMA). The certification expires after ten years, at which time, the diplomate must participate in a re-certification process, involving documentation of continuing education and a re-certification exam.

In as much as the programs offered specifically to medical doctors are much abbreviated and tend to "medicalize" acupuncture by explaining and using it within a western medical paradigm, many professional acupuncturists do not consider this training to be appropriate or adequate to the practice of acupuncture.

Chiropractors

Chiropractic is based in western science and medical philosophy, but it is normally grouped with the so-called complementary and alternative therapies because it is not viewed as conventional medical practice by the medical profession. As mentioned earlier, the chiropractic community has had its share of battles in overcoming the medical profession's resistance to acknowledging the practice of chiropractic as a legitimate healthcare profession. However, the acceptance of chiropractic as a profession began before the practice of acupuncture was recognized as a distinct profession. As a result, not only have acupuncture professionals had to negotiate with the medical community in states where they have passed legislation, they have also had to deal with the chiropractic community in those states as well. Successfully passing a first acupuncture practice act has required compromise in many states. The result is that chiropractors can practice acupuncture within their scope of practice in twenty-eight states, ten of which do not specify any training requirements in acupuncture. In the remaining eighteen states, training requirements are between 100 and 200 hours, but there is no standard curriculum specified.

However, the chiropractic community is the only group of independent healthcare professionals, other than medical doctors, that have created a credentialing process in acupuncture for their members at this time. In recognition of the interest chiropractors have to create a standard for credentialing chiropractors who practice acupuncture within their state scope of practice, the National Board of Chiropractic Examiners (NBCE) has developed a certification exam in acupuncture.

The following information was provided by National Board of Chiropractic Examiners:

The NBCE Acupuncture Examination was developed to assure academic and entry level clinical competence in the area of Clinical Meridian Acupuncture (CMA) as it relates to the practice of chiropractic nationally. The examination is based on the educational components and curricula presented in the acupuncture certification programs of the Council on Chiropractic Education (CCE) colleges and universities and other colleges and universities accredited by agencies recognized by the U.S. Department of Education. The core academic acupuncture curriculum of each of the CCE colleges and universities meets or exceeds the recommendations of the World Federation of Acupuncture Societies (WFAS) of the World Health Organization, for training in acupuncture for physicians. Additionally, the NBCE Acupuncture Examination draws from the internationally accepted text Chinese Acupuncture and Moxibustion, Chen Xinnong, Foreign Language Press, Beijing and the Clean Needle Technique for Acupuncturists, 5th Ed., National Acupuncture Foundation.

Upon satisfactory completion of the prescribed certification programs in acupuncture from an approved college, Doctors of Chiropractic may sit for the NBCE Acupuncture Examination. Through successful performance on this examination, Doctors of Chiropractic earn NBCE recognition for their competence in the practice of acupuncture as an adjunct to chiropractic practice in those states whose scope of chiropractic practice includes acupuncture.

The NBCE exam, specifically, has been adopted by three states so far as an eligibility requirement for a chiropractor to practice acupuncture.

As indicated at the end of the section on the training of medical doctors for acupuncture practice, the education required of chiropractors, where it is required at all, is not considered by many in the acupuncture professional community as adequate for the efficacious practice of acupuncture.

Several other categories of healthcare professionals may practice acupuncture within their scope of practice in various states. Tables 8 and 9 on pages 129-130 are comparative lists by state. In addition to medical doctors and chiropractors, some states have determined acupuncture to be within scope of practice of podiatrists, dentists, physician assistants, naturopathic doctors, optometrists, nurses, physical therapists, and veterinarians. Sometimes training in acupuncture is specified and sometimes not.

Acupuncture Detoxification Specialists

The most widespread use of acupuncture outside of the professional practice of acupuncture is in chemical dependency treatment. Some acupuncture detoxification specialists are licensed acupuncturists, but most are not, and are trained only in a specific acupuncture treatment protocol for use solely in the substance abuse treatment or mental health environment. Acupuncture detoxification specialists may be acupuncturists, physicians, nurses, counselors, social workers, or chemical dependency professionals.

THE REGULATION OF ACUPUNCTURE

The National Acupuncture Detoxification Association (NADA) has led the development of this specialized area of acupuncture practice. It was established in 1985 to promote education and training of the NADA ear acupuncture protocol for the treatment of addiction and mental health disorders. The NADA five-needle ear acupuncture protocol was developed after a Hong Kong neurosurgeon, H.L. Wen M.D., discovered the benefit of acupuncture in alleviating symptoms of drug withdrawal. Eventually, the ear acupuncture protocol developed as an effective supportive treatment method for detoxification, relapse prevention, withdrawal symptoms and a variety of mental health and compulsive behavior disorders. The U.S. National Institutes of Health (NIH) Consensus Panel on acupuncture reviewed the scientific literature and concluded that acupuncture for addiction "may be useful as an adjunct treatment or an acceptable alternative or be included in a comprehensive management program."

In the United States, acupuncture detoxification was first introduced on an outpatient basis in 1974 at Lincoln Hospital, a city facility in the south Bronx area of New York City. In 1987, Bullock, Culliton and Olander published research in the British medical journal, *The Lancet*, on the effectiveness of acupuncture in treating chronic addiction. Since that time, treatment facilities across the U.S. began incorporating acupuncture into their mental health and substance abuse programming.

Understanding the principles of both traditional Oriental medicine and substance abuse is basic to NADA training. The five-point ear acupuncture protocol must be combined with other addiction therapies and meet the professional standards of the field. The combined application of acupuncture with counseling and self-help groups such as Alcoholics Anonymous (AA) and Narcotics Anonymous (NA) enhances opportunities for success. Acupuncture treatment for addictions has been found to be clinically effective, cost-efficient, drug-free and compatible across cultures.

The NADA training is a seventy-hour course in the specific NADA ear acupuncture points and, most importantly, the application of that protocol in a recovery and mental health environment. Completion of the NADA training does not guarantee that a professional will be allowed to practice in their state.

Currently, fourteen states in the United States allow for acupuncture detoxification specialists through statute or administrative rule. Additionally, there are some native American/aboriginal sites that allow for acupuncture detoxification specialists even in states with no regulatory provision. Most of these states require practitioners to be either licensed acupuncturists or NADA-trained practitioners. In virtually all of the states with acupuncture detoxification provisions, the standard of training must meet or exceed the NADA standard.

NADA has been involved in most of the legislative processes regulating the practice of acupuncture detoxification specialists. States that allow for acupuncture detoxification specialists have seen the greatest growth in the use of acupuncture in the addiction and mental health fields. Most states that allow for acupuncture detoxification specialists stipulate that those individuals must be supervised by licensed acupuncturists, or in some cases, by a medical doctor or other designated healthcare practitioner.

According to the 2002 edition of *The Guide to Acu Detox Resources*, published by J&M Reports, L.L.C. there are over 700 program sites in thirty-nine U.S. states and territories. There are also a number of programs in Canada and Mexico. Many European countries have organized NADA associations. NADA founder Dr. Michael O. Smith has been the most prolific of trainers, taking the NADA training not only across the United States, but also to such far away sites as India, Australia, Germany, Italy, Mexico, Nepal, Siberia, Sweden, and the United Kingdom.

It is difficult to say how many professionals have been trained in the NADA protocol. However, NADA counts over 10,000 trained practitioners in the United States, Canada and U.S. territories.

THE REGULATION OF ACUPUNCTURE

Other Aspects of Oriental Medicine

Although the term "acupuncture" may seem to describe only one facet of an entire system of healing, it has come to represent the profession as a whole in the minds of many, particularly state regulators, as noted earlier. The reason why Oriental medicine was not used to describe the profession in its early days stems from the politics of professional regulation. The term "medicine" was, and remains, objectionable to many in the medical community. When crafting legislation, it has been much easier to "sell" acupuncture, a unique technique that could be clearly described, trained for, and separately regulated.

As acupuncture has become increasingly accepted in this country and the professional community has grown in numbers and political strength, there has been movement towards changing the identity of the profession by appending "Oriental medicine" to acupuncture. It is common now to hear the profession referred to as "acupuncture and Oriental medicine (AOM)," at least within the professional community. Most national organizations and state professional organizations have changed their names to include "Oriental medicine." But, how is the professional community defining Oriental medicine and how is this shift affecting regulation of the profession?

Most practitioners of acupuncture and/or Oriental medicine would agree that Oriental medicine is inclusive of all theory and therapies unique to that system of health and healing. However, for the purposes of defining professional standards at this time, the term Oriental medicine denotes the addition of the practice of Chinese herbal medicine to the practice of acupuncture. Although many academic programs now include curricula in Chinese herbal medicine, most students do not study other Oriental medicine therapies and techniques, such as Oriental massage, gwa sha, and medical qigong, to name a few, in any depth.

The NCCAOM offers a separate credential in Chinese herbology, but no state licenses the practice of Chinese herbology separately from acupuncture. In addition, the NCCAOM credential in Chinese herbology alone will not satisfy a state requirement for NCCAOM exam or certification for a license to practice acupuncture. However, the NCCAOM credential in acupuncture alone will satisfy a state requirement for NCCAOM exam or certification for a license to practice acupuncture, even in the majority of states that include herbal medicine in the scope of practice.

Defining Oriental medicine is further complicated by the inclusion in the scope of practice in several states of therapies that are neither acupuncture nor Oriental medicine and/or which are not included in the core curriculum of accredited acupuncture and Oriental medicine academic programs.

Asian Bodywork Therapy/Oriental Massage

One group of healthcare practitioners who practice an aspect of Oriental medicine have pursued independent credentialing outside the realm of professional acupuncture and Oriental medicine. The American Organization for Bodywork Therapies of Asia (AOBTA) was founded in 1989 by leaders of the major American associations and schools of Asian Bodywork Therapy. AOBTA recognizes a broad spectrum of Asian bodywork techniques practiced in the United States today, including Acupressure™, Amma, AMMA Therapy®, Chi Nei Tsang, Five Element Shiatsu, Integrative Eclectic Shiatsu, Japanese Shiatsu, Jin Shin Do® Bodymind Acupressure™, Macrobiotic Shiatsu, Medical Qigong, Nuad Bo Rarn (Thai Bodywork), Shiatsu, Shiatsu Anma Therapy, Tuina and Zen Shiatsu. The AOBTA currently has 1,500 members of which approximately 5% are licensed acupuncturists. The primary practice and licensure for the majority of those in AOBTA or practicing some form of Asian bodywork, is massage.

Interestingly, when Asian bodywork therapists chose to pursue a credentialing process for Asian bodywork, they did not go to the national massage certifying body, but to the NCCAOM. Although Asian bodywork is clearly a massage therapy, those who practice it strongly identify themselves as practitioners of Oriental medicine because the application of the therapy is based on Oriental medicine theory and diagnosis of imbalance in the body and not on Western medical concepts of health and healing. The AOBTA assisted the National Certification Commission for Acupuncture and Oriental Medicine (NCCAOM) in creating a certification exam in Asian Bodywork Therapy. The first NCCAOM diplomates in Asian Bodywork Therapy (ABT) were granted certification in the year 2000. Seven states and the District of Columbia currently accept the NCCAOM exam as a route of licensure to practice massage.

It should be noted that, although the NCCAOM has created a credential for Asian Bodywork Therapy as part of its offerings in Oriental medicine credentialing, the ABT exam is not required for certification in Oriental Medicine.

Conclusion

The regulation of acupuncture and Oriental medicine seems destined to remain a largely disarticulated process. At a critical juncture in its history in this county, the acupuncture and Oriental medicine profession embraced a regulatory system that is flawed and reflects the political nature and critical deficiencies of the healthcare delivery system of which it is a part. Lack of unity within the profession concerning how it identifies and defines itself and lack of consensus on entry-level standards of education indicate that, in spite of increasing acceptance and awareness of acupuncture by the general populace, the path to full integration into American healthcare may be a difficult one.

Chapter Resources

Accreditation Commission for Acupuncture and Oriental Medicine (ACAOM). *(see Resources for full listing)*

American Academy of Medical Acupuncture (AAMA). *(see Resources for full listing)*

American Organization for Bodywork Therapies of Asia (AOBTA).*(see Resources for full listing)*

Blevins, Sue A. 1995. *The Medical Monopoly: Protecting Consumers or Limiting Competition?* Cato Institute. www.cato.org

Cohen, Michael H. 1998. *Complementary & Alternative Medicine: Legal Boundaries and Regulatory Perspectives.* Baltimore & London: Johns Hopkins University Press

Cohen, Michael H. 2000. *Beyond Complementary Medicine: Legal and Ethical Perspectives on Health Care and Human Evolution.* Ann Arbor: The University of Michigan Press

Council of Colleges of Acupuncture and Oriental Medicine (CCAOM). *(see Resources for full listing)*

Federation of Acupuncture and Oriental Medicine Regulatory Agencies (FAOMRA). *(see Resources for full listing)*

Federation of Chiropractic Licensing Boards (FCLB). *(see Resources for full listing)*

National Board of Chiropractice Examiners (NBCE). *(see Resources for full listing)*

National Certification Commission for Acupuncture and Oriental Medicine (NCCAOM). *(see Resources for full listing)*

National Acupuncture Detoxification Association (NADA). *(see Resources for full listing)*

World Health Organization (WHO). *(see Resources for full listing)*

ACUPUNCTURE LAWS & REGULATIONS
STATE-BY-STATE

ALABAMA

Year first statute passed: N/A	**# Licensed Practitioners:** N/A
Statute #: N/A	**Title of license:** N/A
Governing Body: N/A	

There is no practice act for acupuncturists

Information provided by the State Board of Medical Examiners in 2004

Only a medical doctor, osteopath, or chiropractor may practice acupuncture in Alabama.

There are no specific training requirements for a medical doctor or osteopath to practice acupuncture. The Medical Licensure Commission of Alabama Rule 545-X-4-05 mandates that licensed physicians who practice acupuncture must comply with FDA requirements.

An acupuncturist may not practice under M.D. or D.O. supervision.

There is no provision for the practice of acupuncture by chemical dependency specialists.

Information provided by the State Board of Chiropractic Examiners in 2004

A chiropractic physician may practice acupuncture after documentation of 100 hours of acupuncture course work from board approved sources and passage of an exam administered by an approved chiropractic school or college.

Acupuncture is defined in the board rules as a "modality consisting of stimulating various points on or within the human body or interruption of the cutaneous integrity by specific needle insertion."

An acupuncturist may not practice under the supervision of a chiropractor.

ALASKA

Year first statute passed: 1990

Statute #: AS 08.06.010–08.06.190
Regulations: 12 AAC 05.100–05.990

Regulatory Agency Contact:
Ms. P.J. Gingras
Department of Commerce, Community and Economic Development
Division of Occupational Licensing–Acupuncture
PO Box 11086
Juneau, AK 99811-0806
(907) 465-2695
(907) 465-2974 FAX
www.commerce.state.ak.us/occ/

 # Active Licenses: 62

Title of license:
Licensed Acupuncturist

Use of titles:
An acupuncturist may not use the title "physician" unless also licensed as a physician.

Fees: Application $50
Initial License $200
Biennial Renewal $200

Governing Body
Division of Occupational Licensing.

Definition of Acupuncture
According to statute—"acupuncture" means a form of healing developed from traditional Chinese medical concepts that uses the stimulation of certain points on or near the surface of the body by the insertion of needles to prevent or modify the perception of pain or to normalize physiological functions. The "practice of acupuncture" means the insertion of sterile acupuncture needles and the application of moxibustion to specific areas of the human body based upon acupuncture diagnosis; the practice of acupuncture includes adjunctive therapies involving mechanical, thermal, electrical, and electromagnetic treatment and the recommendation of dietary guidelines and therapeutic exercise.

There is no further definition by rule.

Whether the treatment of animals is within the scope of practice of a licensed acupuncturist has not been determined.

Homeopathy is not within the scope of practice of acupuncture. Homeopathy is regulated in Alaska under the practice of naturopathy.

Eligibility Requirements for Licensure
Formal Education Requirements: Completion of a course of study consistent with the core curriculum and guidelines of the National Council of Acupuncture Schools and Colleges at a school approved by the department. Individuals who graduated from a United States non-ACAOM school or are foreign trained may be licensed to practice if they are licensed in another jurisdiction that has licensing requirements equivalent to those of Alaska.

Undergraduate Requirements: None.

ALASKA

Apprenticeship: Not a route of eligibility.

Experience: Not a route of eligibility.

NCCAOM Credentials Documentation Review Accepted: Yes.

Other Eligibility Requirements: An applicant must be of good moral character and at least 21 years of age, have no disciplinary proceedings or unresolved complaints at the time of application, and have had no license suspended or revoked in Alaska or another jurisdiction.

Written Exam: The NCCAOM written examination.

Practical Exam: None specified.

Reciprocity/Endorsement: Individuals who graduated from a United States non-ACAOM school or are foreign trained may be licensed to practice if they are licensed in another jurisdiction that has licensing requirements equivalent to those of Alaska.

Supervision or Referral Requirement

None.

Malpractice Insurance Requirement

Not required. However, practitioners without malpractice insurance are required to disclose that fact to each patient.

Health Insurance Coverage

Neither third party reimbursement nor reimbursement under workers' compensation is mandated.

Chemical Dependency Specialists

There is no provision for the practice of acupuncture by chemical dependency specialists.

Continuing Education Requirement

Upon biennial renewal: 15 contact hours of continuing education.

Practice management courses not accepted.

Distance learning accepted from accredited program.

Practice of Acupuncture by Other Healthcare Providers

Medical doctors, osteopaths, podiatrists, and dentists are exempt from the provisions of the statute.

Information Provided by the State Medical Board in 2004: The board of medicine has not set specific training requirements for the practice of acupuncture by medical doctors.

Information Provided by the Board of Chiropractic Examiners in 2004: Acupuncture is not within the scope of practice of chiropractors.

Notes

Practitioners must disclose their training to all patients before treatment.

ARIZONA

Year first statute passed: 1998

Statute #: Title 32 Chapter 39

Regulatory Agency Contact:
Mr. Allen Imig
Acupuncture Board of Examiners
1400 West Washington, Suite 230
Phoenix, AZ 85007
(602) 542-3095
(602) 542-3093 FAX
www.azacuboard.az.gov

 # Licensed Practitioners: 314

Title of license:
Licensed Acupuncturist

Use of titles:
Licensure as an acupuncturist does not by itself entitle a person to use the title "doctor" or "physician."

Fees:
Application	$150
Initial License	$275
Biennial Renewal	$275

Governing Body

The Acupuncture Board of Examiners consists of four acupuncturists, three consumers and two other health-care professionals.

Definition of Acupuncture

According to statute —*"acupuncture" means puncturing the skin by thin, solid needles to reach subcutaneous structures. Stimulating the needles to affect a positive therapeutic response at a distant site and the use of adjunctive therapies. "Adjunctive therapies" means the manual, mechanical, magnetic, thermal, electrical or electromagnetic stimulation of acupuncture points and energy pathways, auricular and detoxification therapy, ion cord devices, electroacupuncture, herbal poultices, therapeutic exercise and acupressure.*

Whether the treatment of animals is within the scope of practice has not been determined.

Eligibility Requirements for Licensure

Formal Education Requirements: Graduation from or completion of a training in a board-approved program of acupuncture with a minimum of 1,850 hours that includes at least 800 hours of clinical training.

Undergraduate Requirements: None.

Apprenticeship: Rules are being developed.

Experience: Not a route of eligibility.

NCCAOM Credentials Documentation Review Accepted: No.

Other Eligibility Requirements: Completion of a clean needle technique course approved by the board.

Written Exam: The NCCAOM exam or another examination recognized by the board.

Practical Exam: None specified.

Reciprocity/Endorsement: If an applicant is licensed by another state with substantially similar standards, and has not had certification or licensure revoked.

ARIZONA

Supervision or Referral Requirement

None.

Malpractice Insurance Requirement

Professional liability insurance is not mandated.

Health Insurance Coverage

Neither third party reimbursement nor reimbursement under workers' compensation is mandated.

Chemical Dependency Specialists

The board may issue an auricular acupuncture certificate to a person who practices auricular acupuncture for the purpose of treating alcoholism, substance abuse or chemical dependency if the person documents training that meets or exceeds the standards of NADA, has completed a board approved clean needle technique course, and practices under the supervision of a licensed acupuncturist in a program approved by the board. The certification fee is $75 per year.

Continuing Education Requirement

Upon biennial renewal: 15 hours of continuing education. Hours in practice management are accepted with some limitations.

Practice of Acupuncture by Other Healthcare Providers

Information Provided by the State Medical Board in 2000: A medical doctor or osteopathic doctor may practice acupuncture under his or her scope of practice. There are no specific training requirements for the practice of acupuncture by a licensed medical or osteopathic doctor.

A physician assistant may practice acupuncture if statutory requirements are met.

Information Provided by the Board of Chiropractic Examiners in 2004: A chiropractor may practice acupuncture if certified by the board. The rules require a minimum of 100 credit hours of study at an accredited chiropractic college or post-graduate study with an instructor on the active or postgraduate staff of an accredited chiropractic college. A chiropractor must pass the National Board of Chiropractic Examiners examination in acupuncture and pay the certification fee.

The definition includes acupuncture by needle, electrical stimulation, ultrasound, acupressure, laser and auricular therapy. It does not include cupping, moxibustion or cosmetic therapy.

Information Provided by the Naturopathic Physician Board of Medical Examiners in 1992: A naturopath may practice acupuncture under the scope of practice that includes natural means, drugless methods and nonsurgical methods. "Nonsurgical methods means a system of treating without surgical invasion of the human body but does not preclude the use of acupuncture." No specific training requirements have been set.

Notes

Unprofessional conduct includes "deriving a financial interest in products the acupuncturist endorses or recommends to the patient without disclosing to the patient in writing the extent of the financial interest."

ARKANSAS

Year first statute passed: 1997

Statute #: Title 17 Chapter 102

Regulatory Agency Contact:
Arkansas State Board of Acupuncture and
Related Techniques
813 West 3rd Street
Little Rock, AR 72201
(501) 683-3583
(501) 244-2333 FAX
www.asbart.org

***Note: This agency did not respond to requests to
update information. The information provided here is
compiled from previous updates and public documents. Please contact the Board directly for the
most current information.*

 # Licensed Practitioners: 26

Title of license:
Doctor of Oriental Medicine

Use of titles:
The statute states that "acupuncturist" includes
the terms "licensed acupuncturist," "certified
acupuncturist," "acupuncture practitioner," and
"Oriental medicine practitioner."

Fees: Application &
Initial License $250
Biennial Renewal $400

Governing Body

The Arkansas State Board of Acupuncture and Related Techniques consists of five full members and one ex officio member. Three full members must be qualified acupuncturists and two are public members. The ex officio member, who may not vote, must be a medical doctor.

Definition of Acupuncture

According to statute—*acupuncture means the insertion, manipulation, and removal of needles from the body, and the use of other modalities and procedures at specific locations on the body, for the prevention, cure, or correction of a malady, illness, injury, pain, or other condition or disorder by controlling and regulating the flow and balance of energy and functioning of the patient to restore and maintain health, but acupuncture shall not be considered surgery. Oriental medicine includes all traditional and modern diagnostic, prescriptive, and therapeutic methods utilized by practitioners of acupuncture and Oriental medicine world wide.*

Included in scope: ordering of laboratory, radiological and other diagnostic testing, injection therapy, laser therapy, therapeutic exercise, herbs, homeopathic remedies, nutritional and dietary supplements, and counseling.

The treatment of animals is not within the scope of practice.

Eligibility Requirements for Licensure

Formal Education Requirements: Graduation from a four-year academic program in acupuncture and Oriental medicine that meets or exceeds ACAOM standards, or other criteria as found reasonable by the board. The program must include a minimum of 800 hours of supervised clinical practice.

Undergraduate Requirements: None specified

ARKANSAS

Apprenticeship: Not a route of eligibility.

Experience: Not a route of eligibility.

NCCAOM Credentials Documentation Review Accepted: Yes.

Other Eligibility Requirements: None.

Written Exam: A passing score on a board-approved nationally recognized examination on acupuncture and Chinese herbal medicine.

Practical Exam: None specified. The rules allow the board to conduct its own exam.

Reciprocity/Endorsement: No.

Supervision or Referral Requirement

None.

Malpractice Insurance Requirement

Professional liability insurance is not mandated.

Chemical Dependency Specialists

Acupuncture detox specialists must register with the board and are permitted to practice only under the supervision of a Doctor of Oriental Medicine who is licensed by the board. They are permitted to use only the five-point ear protocol of NADA for substance abuse and cannot treat or offer treatment in any other capacity.

Health Insurance Coverage

Neither third party reimbursement nor reimbursement under workers' compensation is mandated.

Continuing Education Requirement

Upon biennial renewal: 24 contact hours of continuing education.

Practice of Acupuncture by Other Healthcare Providers

Nothing in the acupuncture practice act prevents any other class of licensed health care professionals from practicing acupuncture and related techniques when permitted by their state licensing board.

Information Provided by the State Medical Board in 2004: The board of medicine has not set specific training requirements for the practice of acupuncture by medical doctors.

Information Provided by the Board of Chiropractic Examiners in 2004: Acupuncture is not within the scope of practice of chiropractors.

CALIFORNIA

Year first statute passed: 1975

Statute #: California Business & Professions Code, Chapter 12, Sections 4925–4979

Regulatory Agency Contact:
Ms. Marilyn Nielsen
Department of Consumer Affairs
Acupuncture Board
444 North 3rd Street, Suite 260
Sacramento, California 95814
(916) 445-3021
(916) 445-3015 FAX
www.acupuncture.ca.gov

Fees: Application $75
Exam and re-exam $550
Initial License $325*
Biennial Renewal $325

Initial license fee is prorated to applicant's birth month.

 # Licensed Practitioners: 8,566

Title of license:
Licensed Acupuncturist

Use of titles:
It is unprofessional conduct for an acupuncturist to use the title "Doctor" or the abbreviation "Dr." in connection with the practice of acupuncture unless he or she possesses a license or certificate which authorizes such use or possesses an earned doctorate degree from an accredited, approved, or authorized postsecondary educational institution. If a licensee can document proof of a Doctorate in Oriental Medicine, the initials or title must be used in conjunction with further information (i.e., the title of Licensed Acupuncturist. An acceptable example is "Name, O.M.D., L.Ac.")

Governing Body

The California Acupuncture Board consists of nine members: three licensed acupuncturists with at least five years of experience in acupuncture and not licensed as physicians and surgeons, one licensed acupuncturist who is also a faculty member of any board approved acupuncture college, one physician and surgeon licensed in California with two years of experience in acupuncture, and four public members.

Definition of Acupuncture

Business and Professions Code Section 4927(d) states—*acupuncture means the stimulation of a certain point or points on or near the surface of the body by the insertion of needles to prevent or modify the perception of pain or to normalize physiological functions including pain control, for the treatment of certain diseases or dysfunctions of the body and includes the techniques of electroacupuncture, cupping and moxibustion.* Business and Professions Code Section 4937(b) states an acupuncturist may—*perform or prescribe the use of oriental massage, acupressure, breathing techniques, exercise, heat, cold, magnets, nutrition, diet, herbs, plant, animal and mineral products, and dietary supplements to promote, maintain and restore health.*

Eligibility Requirements for Licensure

(THREE ROUTES OF ELIGIBILITY)

1) Formal Education Requirements: An applicant must graduate from a California Acupuncture Board approved school. All students entering an acupuncture and Oriental medicine educational training program prior to January 1, 2005 must complete 2,348 hours (1,548 theoretical hours and 800 clinical hours) in the following areas: Traditional Chinese Medicine (660 hours); Clinical (800 Hours), Western Sciences (558 hours); Herbal (300 hours) and Ethics and Practice Management (30 hours). All students entering an acupuncture and Oriental medicine educational training program after January 1, 2005 must complete 3,000 hours (2,050 theoretical hours and 950 clinical hours) in the following areas: Basis Sciences (350 hours); Oriental Medicine Principals, Theories and Treatment (1,255 hours [includes 450 hours in herbs]); Clinical Medicine, Patient Assessment and Diagnosis (240 hours); Case Management (90 hours); Practice Management (45 hours); Public Health (40 hours); Professional Development (30 hours) and Clinical Practice (950 hours).

Undergraduate Requirements: Satisfactory completion of at least two academic years (60 semester credits/90 quarter credits) of education at the baccalaureate level that is appropriate preparation for graduate level work, or the equivalent from an institution accredited by an agency recognized by the U.S. Secretary of Education.

2) Apprenticeship: By statute a tutorial supervisor must have at least ten years of experience practicing as an acupuncturist, licensed in the State of California for at least five years, and takes no more than two trainees at a time. An acupuncture tutorial provides formal clinical training with supplemental theoretical and didactic instruction. Clinical training consists of a minimum of 2,250 hours and the theoretical and didactic training, consisting of a minimum of 1,548 hours, is obtained in an approved school, or another postsecondary educational institution or a school accredited by a regional accrediting agency authorized by the U.S. Department of Education. A written agreement between the licensed supervisor and trainee must be submitted with the Tutorial Application. Supervision must be on-site.

3) Foreign Equivalency: An applicant who has completed education and training outside the United States shall document that such education and experience meets the same requirements of the California trained applicant. All foreign-trained applicants are required to submit documentation of their education evaluated by a credentials evaluation service that is a member of the National Association of Credentials Evaluation Services, Inc.

Experience: Not a route of eligibility.

NCCAOM Credentials Documentation Review Accepted: No. The California Acupuncture Licensing Examination (CALE) is required.

Other Eligibility Requirements: An applicant must be 18 years old.

Written Exam: An applicant must pass a written examination developed and administered by the California Acupuncture Board. The examination covers five content areas that reflect the current job competencies in the practice of acupuncture in California as follows: (1) Patient Assessment–25%; (2) Developing a Diagnostic Impression–20%; (3) Providing Acupuncture Treatment–29%; (4) Prescribing Herbal Medicinal–17%; and (5) Regulations for Public Health and Safety–9%.

Reciprocity/Endorsement: No.

Malpractice Insurance Requirement

Professional liability insurance is not mandated.

Supervision or referral requirement

None.

Chemical Dependency Specialists

There is no provision for the practice of acupuncture by chemical dependency specialists.

Continuing Education Requirement

Upon biennial renewal: 30 hours of continuing education. The California Acupuncture Board must approve providers and courses.

CALIFORNIA

Health Insurance Coverage

If a company reimburses a physician for acupuncture, it must reimburse licensed acupuncturists working within their scope of practice. Additionally, insurance companies which sell policies in the state must offer acupuncture coverage to clients. This does not apply to health maintenance organizations and self-insured plans.

Coverage for acupuncture is mandated under workers' compensation and Medi-Cal. Official CPT codes have been established for acupuncture, electrical stimulation, cupping and moxibustion. Acupuncturists are physicians under workers' compensation (Labor Code Section 3209.3).

Practice of Acupuncture by Other Healthcare Providers

Nothing in the Acupuncture Licensure Act prevents the practice of acupuncture by a person licensed as a physician and surgeon, a dentist*, or a podiatrist, within the scope of their respective licenses.

Information Provided by the State Medical Board in 2004: The board of medicine has not set specific training requirements for the practice of acupuncture by medical doctors.

Information Provided by the Board of Chiropractic Examiners in 2004: Acupuncture is not within the scope of practice of chiropractors since the chiropractic statute specifies that chiropractors may not penetrate tissue.

Notes

There is provision for guest acupuncturists to engage in professional education through lectures, clinics or demonstrations, for up to a six month period, when visiting in conjunction with a professional acupuncture association, scientific acupuncture foundation, acupuncture training program in a board-approved school, or a continuing education provider. The guest acupuncturist may not set up practice.

There is provision for inactive status. A license must have a current active status before it can be placed on inactive status. While on inactive status the licensee must pay the required renewal fees, but is exempt from completing continuing education as a condition of renewal. Also while on inactive status a practitioner is precluded from practicing. To reactive a license, 30 hours of board-approved continuing education within the past two years of being inactive is required.

The rules specify standards of practice for condition of offices; treatment procedures that include clean needle technique and needle disposal, treatments outside the office, record keeping and advertising.

An acupuncturist may not advertise that acupuncture can "cure" any condition. Also an acupuncturist is not permitted to diagnose, treat, alleviate or cure cancer, however treatments are permitted if it is intended to relieve the side effects of or protect the body from the damaging effects of the therapies used to treat cancer and if it does not counteract the efficacy of or otherwise interfere with the treatments prescribed for the patient by a physician or other person licensed to treat or alleviate cancer.

The 2004 Sunset Review Report and Recommendations, and the report and findings of the Little Hoover Commission may effect changes in regulations within the next year.

*The Dental Board of California issued proposed regulations (affecting Section 1064 of the California Code of Regulations) for 2005 reducing the number of hours required to perform dental acupuncture from 80 hours to 24 hours. The effort was not successful.

COLORADO

Year first statute passed: 1989

Statute #: Title 12–Article 29.5 Colorado Revised Statutes (last revised 2002)

Regulatory Agency Contact:
Mr. Kevin Heupel
Department of Regulatory Agencies
Office of Acupuncturists Licensure
1560 Broadway, Suite 1340
Denver, CO 80202-5140
(303) 894-7429
(303) 894-7764 FAX
www.dora.state.co.us/acupuncturists

 # Licensed Practitioners: 711

Title of license:
Licensed Acupuncturist

Use of titles:
There is no statutory authority to use the title of "doctor." A licensee may use the title "licensed acupuncturist," "registered acupuncturist," or "diplomate of acupuncture," or, use the designation "L.Ac.," "R.Ac.," or "Dipl.Ac."

Fees:* Application and
Initial License $100
Annual Renewal $108

fees are subject to change every two years.

Governing Body

Department of Regulatory Agencies.

Definition of Acupuncture

According to statute, acupuncture is—*a system of health care based on traditional Oriental medical concepts that employs Oriental methods of diagnosis, treatment, and adjunctive therapies for the promotion, maintenance, and restoration of health and the prevention of disease.*

The "practice of acupuncture"—*means the insertion and removal of acupuncture needles, the application of heat therapies to specific areas of the human body, and traditional oriental adjunctive therapies. Traditional Oriental adjunctive therapies within the scope of acupuncture may include manual, mechanical, thermal, electrical, and electromagnetic treatment, the recommendation of Oriental therapeutic exercises, and subject to federal law, the recommendation of herbs and dietary guidelines. The "practice of acupuncture" shall be defined by traditional Oriental medical concepts and shall not include the utilization of western medical diagnostic tests and procedures, such as magnetic resonance imaging, radiographs (x-rays), computerized tomography scans, and ultrasound. "Practice of acupuncture" does not mean osteopathic medicine and osteopathic manipulative treatment, chiropractic or chiropractic adjustment, or physical therapy.*

There is no further definition by rule.

The treatment of animals is not within the scope of practice.

Whether homeopathy is within the scope of practice of acupuncture has not been determined.

Eligibility Requirements for Licensure

Eligibility Requirements: Current, active NCCAOM certification in acupuncture.

COLORADO

Reciprocity/Endorsement: There are two requirements for licensure by endorsement: 1) the NCCAOM must provide the Colorado Office of Acupuncturists Licensure with proof of the applicant's current NCCAOM certification status; 2) Proof of the applicant's licensure in another state must be provided by the licensing authority in that state to the Colorado Office of Acupuncturists Licensure.

Supervision or Referral Requirement

None.

Malpractice Insurance Requirement

Individual acupuncturists must carry 50,000/50,000 professional liability insurance and limited liability companies or corporations must carry 300,000/300,000.

Health Insurance Coverage

Neither third party reimbursement nor reimbursement under workers' compensation is mandated.

Chemical Dependency Specialists

There is no provision for the practice of acupuncture by chemical dependency specialists.

Continuing Education Requirement

None.

Practice of Acupuncture by Other Healthcare Providers

Information Provided by the Board of Medical Examiners in 2004: An M.D. or D.O. may practice acupuncture if the physician believes he or she is trained and competent to do so. However, there is no specific acupuncture training requirements set forth in statute that physicians must have to perform acupuncture.

It has not been determined whether acupuncture is within the scope of practice of podiatry.

Acupuncture is not within the scope of practice of a physician assistant.

Information Provided by the Board of Chiropractic Examiners in 2004: Acupuncture is an optional certification for chiropractors. In order to be certified an individual must show 100 hours of theory and supervised clinical instruction plus affidavits of 25 cases.

Notes

Colorado provides an extensive list of information that must be provided to the patient regarding the acupuncturist's training and background.

CONNECTICUT

Year first statute passed: 1995

Statute #: Chapter 384C

Regulatory Agency Contact:
Ms. Lawanda Scott
Acupuncture Licensing Section
Department of Public Health
410 Capitol Avenue, MS#12 APP
PO Box 340308
Hartford, CT 06134-0308
(860) 509-8388
(860) 509-8457 FAX
www.dph.state.ct.us

 # Licensed Practitioners: 257

Title of license:
Acupuncturist

Use of titles:
An acupuncturist may not use the title "physician" or "doctor" unless also licensed as a physician.

Fees: Application and
Initial License $100
Biennial Renewal $200

Governing Body

Department of Public Health.

Definition of Acupuncture

According to statute —*acupuncture means the treating, by means of mechanical, thermal, or electrical stimulation effected by the insertion of needles or by the application of heat, pressure or electrical stimulation at a point or combination of points on the surface of the body predetermined on the basis of the theory of physiological interrelationship of the body organs with an associated point or combination of points for diseases, disorders and dysfunctions of the body for the purpose of achieving a therapeutic or prophylactic effect but shall not include the practice of physical therapy.*

There is no further definition by rule.

The treatment of animals is not within the scope of practice.

Homeopathy is not within the scope of practice of acupuncture. It is the practice of medicine.

Eligibility Requirements for Licensure

Formal Education Requirements: Successful completion of a course of study in acupuncture in a program which, at the time of graduation, was in candidate status with or accredited by an accrediting agency recognized by the U.S. Department of Education and which included a minimum of 1,350 hours of didactic and clinical training, 500 of which were clinical.

Undergraduate Requirements: 60 semester hours, or its equivalent, of postsecondary study in an institution of postsecondary education, which, if in the United States or its territories, was accredited by a recognized regional accrediting body or, if outside the United States or its territories, was legally chartered to grant postsecondary degrees in the country in which located.

Apprenticeship: Not a route of eligibility.

Experience: Not a route of eligibility.

NCCAOM Credentials Documentation Review Accepted: No.

CONNECTICUT

Written Exam: The NCCAOM written examination.

Practical Exam: The NCCAOM PEPLS examination.

Other Eligibility Requirements: Must have successfully completed a course in clean needle technique prescribed by the department.

Reciprocity/Endorsement: Applicant must present evidence of licensure or certification as an acupuncturist in another state or jurisdiction whose requirements for practice are substantially similar to or higher than those of Connecticut and that there are no disciplinary actions or unresolved complaints pending.

Supervision or Referral Requirement

None.

Malpractice Insurance Requirement

Professional liability insurance is not mandated.

Health Insurance Coverage

Neither third party reimbursement nor reimbursement under workers' compensation is mandated.

Chemical Dependency Specialists

Auricular acupuncture may be performed by individuals certified by an organization approved by the commissioner of public health, provided such person shall perform auricular acupuncture only in a designated site and in accordance with a standard written protocol developed by a physician employed by or designated by the department of public health and addiction services.

Auricular acupuncture is defined as treatment by the insertion of needles at a specified combination of points on the surface of the outer ear for the purpose of facilitating the detoxification and rehabilitation of [substance] alcohol and drug abusers.

Continuing Education Requirement

None.

Practice of Acupuncture by Other Healthcare Providers

Medical doctors, chiropractors, dentists, physical therapists, podiatrists, homeopaths, naturopaths, optometrists, and veterinarians are exempt from the acupuncture licensing statute.

Information Provided by the State Department of Public Health in 2000: No specific training in acupuncture is required for a medical doctor or osteopath to practice acupuncture provided such services are consistent with the appropriate scope of practice.

Acupuncture may be practiced by a physician assistant or nurse under the supervision of a licensed medical doctor. A physician assistant must have graduated from an accredited physician assistant program and pass the national physician assistant examination.

A physical therapist may practice acupuncture provided he or she is licensed as a physical therapist.

The department has stated—"As with any area of medical practice, it is the professional responsibility of the practitioner who elects to perform acupuncture to ensure that she or he has had adequate preparation to perform such services competently."

DELAWARE

Year first statute passed: N/A	**# Licensed Practitioners:** N/A
Statute #: N/A	**Title of license:** N/A
Governing Body: N/A	

There is no practice act for acupuncturists

Information provided by the State Board of Medical Examiners in 2004

According to the Board of Medical Examiners—"a license as a medical doctor is a prerequisite to the practice of acupuncture in Delaware; it falls within the definition of the practice of medicine."

There is no provision for the practice of acupuncture by chemical dependency specialists.

Information provided by the State Board of Chiropractic Examiners in 2004

Acupuncture is within the scope of practice of a chiropractor. Certification in any nationally recognized specialty requires a minimum of 100 or more hours of certified training beyond and in addition to any courses or training received toward the doctor of chiropractic degree.

DISTRICT OF COLUMBIA

Year first statute passed: 1989

Statute #: Title 17, Chapter 47

Regulatory Agency Contact:
Mr. Jim Granger, Jr.
Department of Health
Advisory Committee on Acupuncture
825 North Capitol Street NE, Room 2224
Washington, DC 20002
(202) 442-4777
(202) 442-9431 FAX
www.dchealth.dc.gov

Note: *This agency did not respond to requests to update information. The information provided here is compiled from previous updates and public documents. Please contact the Board directly for the most current information.*

 # Licensed Practitioners: 176

Title of license:
Acupuncturist

Use of titles:
Unless authorized to practice medicine a person shall not use or imply the use of the words or terms "physician," "medical doctor," "M.D.," or any similar title or description of services with the intent to represent that the person practices medicine.

Fees:

Application	$91
Initial License	$111
Biennial Renewal	$111

Governing Body

The Board of Medicine. The Advisory Committee on Acupuncture is supervised by the Board of Medicine.

Definition of Acupuncture

According to statute—*practice of acupuncture means the insertion of needles, with or without accompanying electrical or thermal stimulation, at a certain point or points on or near the surface of the human body to relieve pain, normalize physiological functions, and treat ailments or conditions of the body.*

Eligibility Requirements for Licensure

Formal Education Requirements: Completion of three academic years of instruction in acupuncture including 500 hours of clinic in a school for acupuncture, or two academic years of instruction in a school for acupuncture plus 1,500 hours of apprenticeship. The school must be legally chartered or organized in the state, territory or country where the school is located or accredited or recognized by ACAOM.

Undergraduate Requirements: None specified.

Apprenticeship: A tutorial must be at least three years with a minimum of 4,500 contact hours.

Experience: The board may approve the education and training of an applicant who documents three years of experience prior to October 1989 with a minimum of 100 patients and 500 patient visits each year in general healthcare.

NCCAOM Credentials Documentation Review Accepted: No.

Written Exam: The NCCAOM written exam. An applicant may not fail the NCCAOM exam more than six times.

Practical Exam: The NCCAOM exam, or a practical exam administered by the board.

DISTRICT OF COLUMBIA

Other Eligibility Requirements: An applicant who does not speak English as a native language must receive a passing score on an English competency test approved by the board. The rules do not specify a particular test or score.

Reciprocity/Endorsement: All applicants for reciprocity must have passed the NCCAOM exam.

Supervision or Referral Requirement

Effective July 8, 2004—*a licensed acupuncturist does not need to enter into a collaborating agreement with a licensed physician or osteopath.*

Chemical Dependency Specialists

There is no provision for the practice of acupuncture by chemical dependency specialists.

Malpractice Insurance Requirement

Professional liability insurance is not mandated.

Continuing Education Requirement

None.

Practice of Acupuncture by Other Healthcare Providers

Information Provided by the Board of Medicine in 1998: Medical doctors, osteopaths, and chiropractors must have 250 hours of acupuncture instruction from a program approved by the board in order to practice acupuncture.

Health Insurance Coverage

Neither third party reimbursement nor reimbursement under workers' compensation is mandated.

FLORIDA

Year first statute passed: 1981

Statute #: Florida Statutes 457, Rule Chapter 64B1

Regulatory Agency Contact:
Ms. Ronda Bryan
Division of Medical Quality Assurance
Board of Acupuncture
4052 Bald Cypress Way
Bin #C06
Tallahassee, FL 32399
(850) 245-4586
(850)921-6184 FAX
www.doh.state.fl.us/mqa/acupuncture/
acu_home.html

 # Licensed Practitioners: 1,580

Title of license:
Acupuncture Physician

Use of titles:
By Board rule:
L.A.c - Licensed Acupuncturist
R.Ac. - Registered Acupuncturist
A.P. - Acupuncture Physician
D.O.M. - Doctor of Oriental Medicine

Fees:

Application	$300
Initial License	$400
Biennial Renewal	$300
Unlicensed Activity Fee	$5

Governing Body

The Board of Acupuncture consists of seven members: five certified acupuncturists and two lay persons, all appointed by the governor.

Definition of Acupuncture

According to statute—*"acupuncture" means a form of primary health care, based on traditional Chinese medical concepts and modern Oriental medical techniques, that employs acupuncture diagnosis and treatment, as well as adjunctive therapies and diagnostic techniques, for the promotion, maintenance, and restoration of health and the prevention of disease. Acupuncture shall include, but not be limited to, the insertion of acupuncture needles and the application of moxibustion to specific areas of the human body. "Oriental medicine" means the use of acupuncture, electro-acupuncture, Qi Gong, Oriental massage, herbal therapy, dietary guidelines, and other adjunctive therapies.*

The treatment of animals is not within the scope of practice.

Eligibility Requirements for Licensure

Formal Education Requirements: Completion of a three-year course of study in acupuncture and Oriental medicine, and effective July 1, 2001, a four-year course of study in acupuncture and Oriental medicine, which meets standards established by the board by rule, which standards include, but are not limited to, western anatomy, western physiology, western pathology, western biomedical terminology, first aid, and cardiopulmonary resuscitation (CPR). However, any person who enrolled in an authorized course of study in acupuncture before August 1, 1997, must have completed only a two-year course of study which meets standards established by the board by rule, which standards must include, but are not limited to, successful completion of academic courses in western anatomy, western physiology, and western pathology.

FLORIDA

The rules require that applicants who apply for licensure on or after October 1, 2003 must have graduated from an ACAOM candidate or accredited four-year master's level program or foreign equivalent in Oriental medicine with a minimum of 2,700 hours of supervised instruction; 2 hours of medical errors; 15 hours of universal precautions; 3 hours of HIV/AIDS, and 20 hours in Florida statutes and rules.

Undergraduate Requirements: 60 college credits.

Apprenticeship: Not a route of eligibility.

Experience: Not a route of eligibility.

Other Eligibility Requirements: An applicant must be at least 18 years old and a U.S. citizen, permanent resident or legal alien in the U.S. for six months prior to the date of application.

Written Examination: The board currently approves as the Florida examination for licensure the NCCAOM written examinations consisting of the Foundations of Oriental Medicine Module and the Acupuncture Module.

Practical Examination: The NCCAOM Point Location Module.

Reciprocity/Endorsement: Endorsement is possible if an applicant is "actively licensed in a state which has examination requirements that are substantially equivalent to or more stringent than Florida," or has completed a national certification process. However, all applicants must also meet the educational and general eligibility requirements for licensure.

Chemical Dependency Specialists

Acupuncture for chemical dependency may only be practiced by certified acupuncturists.

Health Insurance Coverage

A company which reimburses any healthcare provider for acupuncture treatment must reimburse a licensed acupuncturist.

Continuing Education Requirement

Upon biennial renewal: 30 total hours of continuing education in the following areas:

Medical Errors:	2 hours
HIV/AIDS	2 hours
Laws & Rules	2 hours
Laboratory Test Findings	2 hours
Imaging Findings	2 hours
General	16 hours

Note: Effective for the biennium beginning March 1, 2004, and ending February 28, 2006, all non-statutory continuing education licensure renewal requirements imposed by board rule are suspended. No continuing education credits will be required for renewal of licensure at the February 28, 2006 renewal date except for the medical errors and HIV/palliative care requirements imposed by Sections 456.013(7) and 456.033, F.S., respectively.

Practice of Acupuncture by Other Healthcare Providers

Information Provided by the Board of Medical Examiners in 2004:—*The scope of practice of medicine. . .includes the use of acupuncture theories, therapies and modalities by any licensee who has received education and training in the medical uses of such theories, therapies and modalities.* (64B8-2.003)

Information Provided by the Board of Chiropractic in 2004: Acupuncture is an optional certification examination for chiropractic physicians. They may practice acupuncture with 100 hours of board approved training and successful passage of the acupuncture certification examination administered by the National Board of Chiropractic Examiners, but may not advertise themselves as "acupuncturists," only "board certified in acupuncture."

FLORIDA

Malpractice Insurance Requirement

Acupuncturists must carry at least a $30,000 bond or professional liability insurance policy.

Supervision or Referral Requirement

None.

Notes

Provision is made for inactive status. Extensive infection control regulations are specified. Types of required medical record keeping are stated in the rules. AIDS and medical errors coursework are required to receive, renew, or reactivate a license.

GEORGIA

Year first statute passed: 2000

Statute #: 43-34-60 through 43-34-72

Regulations: Chapter 360-6 Acupuncture

Regulatory Agency Contact:
Ms. LaSharn Hughes
Georgia Board of Medical Examiners
2 Peachtree Street NW
Atlanta, GA 30303-3159
(404) 656-3913
(404) 656-9723 FAX
www.sos.state.ga.us/ebd-medical

 # Licensed Practitioners: 132

Title of license:
Licensed Acupuncturist

Use of titles:
An acupuncture detox specialist may not use the title "Acupuncturist" or "Licensed Acupuncturist."

Fees: Application $300
       Biennial Renewal $150

Governing Body

Board of Medical Examiners. An advisory committee to the board must have at least two members who are licensed acupuncturists.

Definition of Acupuncture

According to statute—*"acupuncture" means a form of therapy developed from traditional and modern Oriental concepts for health care that employs Oriental medical techniques, treatment, and adjunctive therapies for the promotion, maintenance and restoration of health and the prevention of disease. "Practice of acupuncture" means the insertion of disposable acupuncture needles and the application of moxibustion to specific areas of the human body based upon Oriental medical principles as a therapeutic modality. Adjunctive therapies within the scope of acupuncture may include manual, mechanical, herbal, thermal, electrical, and electromagnetic treatment and the recommendation of dietary guidelines and exercise, but only if such treatments, recommendations, and exercises are based on concepts of traditional Oriental medicine and are directly related to acupuncture therapy.*

Eligibility Requirements for Licensure

An applicant must be NCCAOM certified in acupuncture, complete a national recognized clean needle technique course approved by the board, and be at least 21 years of age. A grandparenting provision is included for individuals who practiced in the state prior to the passage of the law.

Malpractice Insurance Requirement

Acupuncturists must have professional liability insurance in the amount of at least $100,000/$300,000

Continuing Education Requirement

None.

GEORGIA

Supervision or Referral Requirement

None, unless the licensee has less than one year of clinical experience.

Individuals who have less than one year of postgraduate clinical experience must be supervised for one year by a licensed acupuncturist with a minimum of four years of active licensed practice. The supervising acupuncturist shall be currently licensed in Georgia and actively practicing in Georgia and shall have four years of active licensed clinical experience.

Practice of Acupuncture by Other Healthcare Providers

Information Provided by the Composite State Board of Medical Examiners in 2004: M.D.s or D.O.s approved prior to August 1, 2000 were required to demonstrate at least 100 hours of acupuncture training acceptable to the board in order to practice acupuncture. After that date, they must have successfully completed a board-approved 300-hour course to practice acupuncture, or to practice auricular detox acupuncture, have successfully completed a board-approved course.

Information Provided by the Board of Chiropractic Examiners in 2000: Chiropractors may not practice acupuncture.

Health Insurance Coverage

Neither third party reimbursement nor reimbursement under workers' compensation is mandated.

Chemical Dependency Specialists

According to statute—*"Auricular (ear) detoxification therapy" means the insertion of disposable acupuncture needles into the five auricular acupuncture points stipulated by the National Acupuncture Detoxification Association protocol for the sole purpose of treatment of chemical dependency.*

The practice of auricular detoxification therapy may take place in a city, county, state, federal, or private chemical dependency program approved by the board under the direct supervision of a licensed acupuncturist or a person authorized to practice acupuncture by the board who is also authorized to practice medicine.

Applicants for certification as an acupuncture detoxification specialist must be at least 21 and have successfully completed a nationally recognized training program in auricular (ear) detoxification therapy for the treatment of chemical dependency as approved by the board, and have successfully completed a nationally recognized clean needle technique course approved by the board.

Notes

The statute requires that patients be informed in general terms of the following: (1) That the practice of acupuncture is based upon the Oriental arts and is completely distinct and different from traditional western medicine; (2) That the acupuncturist cannot practice medicine, is not making a medical diagnosis of the person's disease or condition, and that such person should see a physician if he or she wants to obtain medical diagnosis; and (3) The nature and the purpose of the acupuncture treatment.

HAWAII

Year first statute passed: 1974

Statute #: 436E, Hawaii Revised Statutes

Regulatory Agency Contact:
Ms. Christine Rutkowski
Department of Commerce and Consumer Affairs
Professional and Vocational Licensing Division
Board of Acupuncture
PO Box 3469
Honolulu, HI 96801
(808) 586-3000 (application information)
FAX: not available
www.state.hi.us/dcca

Fees: Application $50
        Biennial renewal $220

 # Licensed Practitioners: 532

Title of license:
Licensed Acupuncturist

Use of titles:
The title "Ph.D." is allowed to designate a non-practitioner if it has been awarded by a university or college recognized by a regional or national accrediting body recognized by the U.S. Department of Education. The title "Doctor," or the initials "Dr." or "D.Ac." are allowed if the licensee has been awarded an earned doctorate degree from a university or college recognized by a regional or national accrediting body recognized by the U.S. Department of Education. "Acupuncturist" must follow the person's name.

Governing Body

The Board of Acupuncture consists of two private citizens and three licensed acupuncturists.

Definition of Acupuncture

According to statute—*practice of acupuncture means stimulation of a certain acupuncture point or points on the human body for the purpose of controlling and regulating the flow and balance of energy in the body. The practice includes the techniques of piercing the skin by inserting needles and point stimulation by the use of acupressure, electrical, mechanical, thermal, or traditional therapeutic means.*

The rules include the use of herbal medicine.

The treatment of animals is not within the scope of practice.

Homeopathy is not within the scope of practice of acupuncture. Whether it is the practice of medicine has not been determined.

Eligibility Requirements for Licensure

Formal Education Requirements: An applicant must show completion of a formal acupuncture program, that resulted in the award of a certificate or diploma from an institute, school, or college that is accredited or recognized as a candidate for accreditation by the U.S. Department of Education, or at a foreign institute, school, or college with a formal program in the science of acupuncture, licensed, approved, or accredited by the appropriate governmental authority in that jurisdiction and whose curriculum is approved by the board. The program must consist of at least 2,175 academic and clinical training. The academic program must be at least 1,515 in the science of acupuncture (traditional Oriental medicine) and the clinical program must be at least 660 hours under the supervision of a licensed acupuncturist. These requirements became effective on September 1, 2000.

HAWAII

Undergraduate Requirements: None.

Apprenticeship: None.

Experience: Not a route of eligibility.

NCCAOM Credentials Documentation Review Accepted: No.

Other Eligibility Requirements: None.

Written Exam: Hawaii administers the NCCAOM written examination. The board will waive the NCCAOM exam if taken in another state and the score or passage of the exam is verified directly to the board by the NCCAOM or the licensing state that administered the exam. The NCCAOM exam may be taken in a language other than English. (Note: the Hawaii jurisprudence exam has been discontinued.)

Practical Exam: None specified.

Reciprocity/Endorsement: No.

Supervision or Referral Requirement

Referral by a medical doctor or dentist is required for organic disorders.

No referral is required for pain relief and treatment of functional disorders. Functional disorders are defined as "a condition of the human body in which the symptoms cannot be referred to any organic lesion or change of structure; opposed to organic disorder."

Chemical Dependency Specialists

There is no provision for the practice of acupuncture by chemical dependency specialists.

Health Insurance Coverage

Neither third party reimbursement nor reimbursement under workers' compensation is mandated.

Continuing Education Requirement

None.

Practice of Acupuncture by Other Healthcare Providers

Information Provided by the Board of Medical Examiners in 2004: Medical doctors, osteopaths and physician assistants who desire to practice acupuncture must be licensed under the law governing acupuncture.

It has not been determined whether acupuncture is within the scope of practice of podiatrists.

Information Provided by the Board of Chiropractic Examiners in 2004: A chiropractor who desires to practice acupuncture must be licensed under the law governing acupuncture.

Malpractice Insurance Requirement

Professional liability insurance is not mandated.

Notes

Use of staples is prohibited.

IDAHO

Year first statute passed: 1999	**# Licensed Practitioners:** 75
Statute #: 54-4701-4713	**Title of license:** Licensed Acupuncturist
Regulatory Agency Contact: Ms. Sandee Hitesman Bureau of Occupational Licenses Board of Acupuncture 1109 Main Street, Suite 220 Boise, ID 83702-5642 (208) 334-3233 (208) 334-3945 FAX www.ibol.idaho.gov/acu.htm	**Use of titles:** Persons licensed pursuant to this chapter may use the title "licensed acupuncturist." Individuals may not use the title "doctor" or any abbreviation thereof, unless otherwise authorized to use the title.

Fees:

Application	$250
Initial License	$250
Annual Renewal	$250

Governing Body

The Board of Acupuncture consists of five members: three licensed acupuncturists, one certified acupuncturist and one public member.

Definition of Acupuncture

According to statute—*"acupuncture" means that theory of healthcare developed from traditional and modern Oriental medical philosophies that employs diagnosis and treatment of conditions of the human body based upon stimulation of specific acupuncture points on meridians of the human body for the promotion, mainte-nance, and restoration of health for the prevention of disease. Therapies within the scope of acupuncture include manual, mechanical, thermal, electrical, and electromagnetic treatment of such specific indicated points. Adjunctive therapies included in, but not exclusive to, acupuncture include herbal and nutritional treat-ments, therapeutic exercise and other therapies based on traditional and modern Oriental medical theory. "Practice of acupuncture" means the insertion of acupuncture needles and use of similar devices and ther-apies, including application of moxibustion, to specific indicated points on the skin of the human body as indi-cated pursuant to traditional and modern theories of Oriental medicine. The "practice of acupuncture" does not include: (a) surgery; or (b) prescribing, dispensing or administering any prescription drugs or legend drug as defined in section 54-1705(27), Idaho Code.*

The scope of practice varies with the training of the practitioner. Rule 400 states, "Upon being granted a license or certification to practice acupuncture, a practitioner is authorized to provide only acupuncture serv-ices and treatments for which that practitioner has been appropriately trained and prepared by board-approved education or practical experience."

The treatment of animals is not within the scope of practice of acupuncture.

Homeopathy is not a regulated practice in Idaho. It is not specified within the scope of practice of acupunc-ture. It is not considered to be the practice of medicine.

IDAHO

Eligibility Requirements for Licensure

An applicant must meet NCCAOM eligibility criteria for certification in acupuncture or similar requirements approved by the board, successfully complete an acupuncture internship or equivalent experience approved by the board, obtain a passing grade on an examination (i.e. NCCAOM) or other demonstration of proficiency as required by the board, and successfully complete a blood borne pathogen course and comprehensive examination that incorporates clean needle techniques and OSHA procedures and requirements.

Reciprocity/Endorsement: The board may grant a license to individuals who are currently licensed in acupuncture in another state, the District of Columbia, or a territory of the U.S. which has requirements equivalent to Idaho requirements.

Practice of Acupuncture by Other Healthcare Providers

The statute provides for "acupuncture technicians." Acupuncture technicians must complete the requirements for clinical technician certificate by the International Academy of Medical Acupuncture, Inc., or other such requirements as approved by the board, pass a clean needle technique course approved by the board, and pass an examination or other demonstration of proficiency approved by the board. The board may require that an acupuncture technician practice only under the supervision of a person licensed or certified in acupuncture, and may restrict practice to specified therapies or treatments. Persons certified or granted an acupuncture technician certificate pursuant to this chapter may use the title "certified acupuncturist" or "acupuncture technician" respectively, but may not use the title "licensed acupuncturist" or "doctor," or any abbreviation thereof, unless the acupuncturist is otherwise authorized to use such title.

Information Provided by the State Board of Medicine in 2004: Medical doctors may practice acupuncture under their scope of practice without training. They may seek acupuncture certification through the acupuncture board on a voluntary basis.

Information Provided by the Board of Chiropractic Physicians in 2004: Chiropractors must meet

Practice of Acupuncture by Other Healthcare Providers, continued. . .

educational requirements and be "Certified Acupuncturists" under the Board of Acupuncture in order to practice acupuncture.

Continuing Education Requirement

Upon annual renewal: 15 hours of continuing education.

Supervision or Referral Requirement

None.

Chemical Dependency Specialists

It is unclear whether chemical dependency specialists may be licensed under the Acupuncture Technician provision.

Malpractice Insurance Requirement

Professional liability insurance is not mandated.

Health Insurance Coverage

Neither third party reimbursement nor reimbursement under workers' compensation is mandated.

Notes

See proposed new 2005 regulations: www.ibol.idaho.gov/ACU/acu%20prop%20rules.htm

ILLINOIS

Year first statute passed: 1997

Statute #: 225 Illinois Compiled Statutes 2/1–2/999

Regulatory Agency Contact:
Ms. Sandra Dunn
Illinois Department of Professional Regulation
320 West Washington Street, 3rd Floor
Springfield, IL 62786
(217) 782-8556
(217) 524-2169 FAX
(217) 524-6735 TDD
www.ildfpv.com

Fees: Application $500
        Biennial Renewal $500

 # Licensed Practitioners: 421

Title of license:
Acupuncturist

Use of titles:
No person may use the title and designation of "acupuncturist," "licensed acupuncturist," "certified acupuncturist," "C.A.," "Act.," "Lic.Act.," or "Lic.Ac." unless he or she has been issued registration as an acupuncturist. No person registered as an acupuncturist may use the designation "medical," directly or indirectly in connection with his or her profession or business.

Nothing shall prevent a physician from using the designation "acupuncturist."

Governing Body

Department of Professional Regulation. A seven-person advisory board consists of four acupuncturists that hold an active license to engage in the practice of acupuncture in Illinois, one chiropractic physician licensed under the Medical Practice Act who is actively engaged in the practice of acupuncture, one medical doctor licensed to practice medicine in all of its branches in Illinois and one public member who has no connection with the profession.

Definition of Acupuncture

According to statute—*"acupuncture" means the evaluation or treatment of persons affected through a method of stimulation of a certain point or points on or immediately below the surface of the body by the insertion of pre-sterilized, single-use, disposable needles, unless medically contraindicated, with or without the application of heat, electronic stimulation, or manual pressure to prevent or modify the perception of pain, to normalize physiological functions, or for the treatment of certain diseases or dysfunctions of the body. Acupuncture does not include radiology, electrosurgery, chiropractic technique, physical therapy, naprapathic technique, use or prescribing of any drugs, medications, herbal preparations, nutritional supplements, serums, or vaccines, or determination of a differential diagnosis.*

No further definition by rule.

Eligibility Requirements for Licensure

Eligibility Requirements: NCCAOM certification in acupuncture, passage of a clean needle technique course, good moral character, and at least 18 years of age.

Reciprocity/Endorsement: Endorsement is possible for applicants who are licensed in another state under laws substantially equal to the requirements in force in Illinois on that date.

ILLINOIS

Supervision or Referral Requirement

None.

ed.~the supervision requirement was removed in 2004.

Chemical Dependency Specialists

There is no provision for the practice of acupuncture by chemical dependency specialists.

Malpractice Insurance Requirement

Professional liability insurance is not mandated.

Health Insurance Coverage

Neither third party reimbursement nor reimbursement under workers' compensation is mandated.

Continuing Education Requirement

Beginning with the June 30, 2005 biennial renewal, every licensee who applies for renewal of a license as an acupuncturist shall complete 30 hours of continuing education relevant to the practice of acupuncture.

Practice of Acupuncture by Other Healthcare Providers

A physician or dentist licensed in Illinois may practice acupuncture.

Information Provided by the Department of Professional Regulation in 2004: No specific training is required by a medical doctor, osteopath, or chiropractor to practice acupuncture.

A physician assistant may not perform acupuncture even under supervision.

INDIANA

Year first statute passed: 1999

Statute #: IC 25-2.5

Regulatory Agency Contact:
Ms. Angela Smith-Jones, J.D.
Health Professions Bureau
Medical Licensing Board
402 West Washington, Room 041
Indianapolis, IN 46204
(317) 234-2060
(317) 233-4236 FAX
www.state.in.us/hpb/

 # Licensed Practitioners: 48

Title of license:
Licensed Acupuncturist

Use of titles:
Individuals may not use the title "licensed acupuncturist" or "acupuncturist" unless they are licensed under the acupuncture practice act. Acupuncturists may not use "doctor," "physician," or "surgeon," per IC 25-22.5 of the Medical Practice Act.

Fees: Application $150
  Biennial Renewal $100

Governing Body

Medical Licensing Board. An advisory committee established under the Medical Licensing Board to recommend rules consists of one chiropractor, one podiatrist, one dentist, one acupuncturist and one physician who is a member of the American Academy of Medical Acupuncture.

Definition of Acupuncture

According to statute—*"acupuncture" means a form of health care employing traditional and modern Oriental medical concepts, Oriental medical diagnosis and treatment, and adjunctive therapies and diagnostic techniques for the promotion, maintenance, and restoration of health and the prevention of disease. "Practice of acupuncture" means the insertion of acupuncture needles, the application of moxibustion to specific areas of the human body based upon Oriental medical diagnosis as a primary mode of therapy, and other means of applying acupuncture under this chapter.*

The treatment of animals is not within the scope of practice.

Homeopathy is not within the scope of practice of acupuncture.

Eligibility Requirements for Licensure

Formal Education Requirements: Successful completion of a three-year postsecondary training program or acupuncture college program that is approved by ACAOM.

Undergraduate Requirements: None.

Apprenticeship: Must meet NCCAOM requirements.

Experience: Not a route of eligibility.

NCCAOM Credentials Documentation Review Accepted: Undetermined.

Other Eligibility Requirements: Current active diplomate status with the NCCAOM and completion of a clean needle technique course approved by the NCCAOM.

INDIANA

Reciprocity/Endorsement: An individual who is licensed to practice acupuncture in another state or authorized in another country under qualifications substantially equivalent to those in Indiana may be granted licensure.

Supervision or Referral Requirement

A licensed acupuncturist must obtain a written letter of referral, written diagnosis of the patient, or written documentation relating to the condition for which the patient receives acupuncture within the twelve months immediately preceding the date of the acupuncture.

Practice of Acupuncture by Other Healthcare Providers

Information Provided by the Health Professions Bureau in 2004: Acupuncture is within the scope of practice of licensed medical doctors and osteopaths. No training is specified.

Chiropractors, dentists, and podiatrists may be granted a license to practice acupuncture if they complete at least 200 hours of acupuncture training approved by the board. The board will compile a list of approved training programs. The title of this license is "Licensed Professional Acupuncturist."

Acupuncture is not within the scope of practice of a physician assistant.

Continuing Education Requirement

Upon biennial renewal: an acupuncturist must submit proof of current active NCCAOM certification in acupuncture.

Malpractice Insurance Requirement

Professional liability insurance is not mandated.

Health Insurance Coverage

Neither third party reimbursement nor reimbursement under workers' compensation is mandated.

Chemical Dependency Specialists

Acupuncture detoxification specialists may practice under the supervision of a licensed acupuncturist or physician within the context of a state, federal, or board-approved alcohol, substance abuse, or chemical dependency program upon approval by the board. Training must meet or exceed NADA standards and include completion of a clean needle technique course approved by NCCAOM or NADA. ADS certification is $10, biennial renewal fee is $20.

IOWA

Year first statute passed: 1993

Statute #: 148E

Rules: IAC 653-Chapter 17

Regulatory Agency Contact:
Ms. Amy Van Maanen
Iowa Board of Medical Examiners
400 SW 8th Street, Suite C
Des Moines, IA 50309-4686
(515) 281-6492
(515) 242-5908 FAX
www.docboard.org/ia/acup.htm

 # Licensed Practitioners: 27

Title of license:
Licensed Acupuncturist

Use of titles:
An acupuncturist may only use the tittle "licensed acupuncturist."

Fees: Application fee $ 300
           Biennial renewal $ 300

Governing Body

Board of Medical Examiners.

Definition of Acupuncture

According to statute—*"acupuncture" means a form of healthcare developed from traditional and modern Oriental medical concepts that employs Oriental medical diagnosis and treatment, and adjunctive therapies and diagnostic techniques, for the promotion, maintenance, and restoration of health and the prevention of disease.*

The treatment of animals is not within the scope of practice.

Homeopathy is not within the scope of practice of acupuncture.

Eligibility Requirements for Licensure

Formal Education Requirements: Completion of a three-year postsecondary training program or acupuncture college program which is accredited by, in candidacy for accreditation, or which meets the standards of the National Accreditation Commission for Schools and Colleges of Acupuncture and Oriental Medicine *(ed.~the name of this agency is now the Accreditation Commission for Acupuncture and Oriental Medicine— ACAOM).*

Undergraduate Requirements: None.

Apprenticeship: None.

Experience: None.

NCCAOM Credentials Documentation Review Accepted: No.

Other Eligibility Requirements: Applicants must hold a current active-status NCCAOM certificate in acupuncture or Oriental medicine. Applicants must demonstrate sufficient knowledge of the English language to understand and be understood by patients, medical evaluators, and board and committee members. An applicant who passes the NCCAOM exam in English may be presumed to have sufficient proficiency in English. The board may choose any of the following exams to test the English proficiency of any other applicant: the TOEFL or TSE.

IOWA

Written Exam: The NCCAOM comprehensive written examination including the acupuncture theory and clean needle technique portions are required.

Practical Exam: The NCCAOM PEPLS.

Reciprocity/Endorsement: No.

Supervision or Referral Requirement

None.

Continuing Education Requirement

Upon biennial renewal: 30 hours of continuing education coursework approved by NCCAOM.

Malpractice Insurance Requirement

Professional liability insurance is not mandated.

Health Insurance Coverage

Neither third party reimbursement nor reimbursement under workers' compensation is mandated.

Chemical Dependency Specialists

There is no provision for the practice of acupuncture by chemical dependency specialists.

Practice of Acupuncture by Other Healthcare Providers

Information Provided by the Board of Medical Examiners in 2004: A medical doctor or osteopath may practice acupuncture without specific training in acupuncture.

A physician assistant may not practice acupuncture.

Dentists and podiatrists may practice acupuncture without having an acupuncture license.

Information Provided by the Board of Chiropractic Examiners in 2004: Acupuncture is within the scope of practice of chiropractic. A chiropractic physician must complete 100 hours of classroom instruction, and the certification examination given by a board-approved continuing education sponsor for acupuncture.

Notes

Only presterilized, disposable needles may be used.

A licensed acupuncturist is held to the same standard of care as a person licensed to practice medicine and surgery, osteopathy, or osteopathic medicine and surgery.

KANSAS

Year first statute passed: N/A	**# Licensed Practitioners:** N/A
Statute #: N/A	**Title of license:** N/A
Governing Body: N/A	

There is no practice act for acupuncturists

Information provided by the State Board of Healing Arts in 2004

An acupuncturist may practice under the supervision of, by order of, or referral by a medical doctor, osteopathic doctor, or chiropractic doctor.

A medical doctor, osteopath, or podiatrist may practice acupuncture under his or her scope of practice. While no specific training is identified as a prerequisite to practicing acupuncture, any licensee, whether an M.D., D.O. or D.C., must be competent to perform the treatment. Physician assistants may practice acupuncture if authorized by the physician.

Chiropractors may practice acupuncture. No specific training or course work has been set, but the practitioner must be competent to perform the treatment.

Naturopaths may practice "naturopathic acupuncture" if they have obtained a specialty certification issued by the board.

There is no provision for the practice of acupuncture by chemical dependency specialists.

KENTUCKY

Year first statute passed: N/A	**# Licensed Practitioners:** N/A
Statute #: N/A	**Title of license:** N/A
Governing Body: N/A	

There is no practice act for acupuncturists

Information Provided by the Board of Medical Licensure in 2004

The practice of acupuncture constitutes the practice of medicine and as such may only be engaged in by licensed physicians. Licensed physicians may not employ unlicensed practitioners and therefore may not supervise acupuncturists.

There is no provision for the practice of acupuncture by chemical dependency specialists.

Information Provided by the Board of Chiropractic Examiners in 2004

Acupuncture is not within the scope of practice of chiropractors. Thus a chiropractor also may not supervise acupuncture.

Miscellaneous Notes

A new state professional society plans to introduce legislation in 2005.

LOUISIANA

Year first statute passed: 1975

Statute #: LA. R.S. 37:1356 — 37:1360

Regulatory Agency Contact:
Ms. Sandra Broussard
Louisiana State Board of Medical Examiners
630 Camp Street
PO Box 30250
New Orleans, LA 70112-1449
(504) 568-6820 ext 227
(504) 599-0503 FAX
www.lsbme.org

 # Licensed Practitioners: 12

Title of license:
Acupuncturists' Assistant

Use of titles:
The title of Acupuncturist is used by licensed medical doctors who have been certified in acupuncture. The title of license for non-M.D. acupuncturists is "acupuncturists' assistant."

Fees: Initial License $100
          Annual Renewal $25

Governing Body

Board of Medical Examiners.

Definition of Acupuncture

According to statute—*acupuncture means treatment by means of mechanical, thermal, or electrical stimulation effected by the insertion of needles at a point or combination of points on the surface of the body predetermined on the basis of the theory of the physiological interrelationship of body organs with an associated point or combination of points, or the application of heat or electrical stimulation to such point or points, for the purpose of inducing anesthesia, relieving pain, or healing diseases, disorders and dysfunctions of the body, or achieving a therapeutic or prophylactic effect with respect thereto.*

Also in the statute—*The practice of acupuncture shall be construed to be the practice of medicine.*

The treatment of animals is not within the scope of practice.

Homeopathy is not within the scope of practice of acupuncture.

Eligibility Requirements for Licensure

Formal Education Requirements: An applicant to be an acupuncturists' assistant must successfully complete thirty-six months of training in a school or clinic of traditional Chinese acupuncture approved by the board.

Undergraduate Requirements: None specified.

Apprenticeship: A person may be certified by the board as an acupuncturists' assistant if they have "successfully completed thirty-six months training in a. . .clinic of traditional Chinese acupuncture approved by the board."

Experience: An individual who "has been appointed or employed at a licensed or accredited Louisiana hospital, medical school, or clinic to perform acupuncture for research purposes" may be certified by the board as an acupuncturists' assistant.

NCCAOM Credentials Documentation Review Accepted: No.

LOUISIANA

Other Eligibility Requirements: None.

Written Exam: None specified.

Practical Exam: None specified.

Reciprocity/Endorsement: No.

Supervision or Referral Requirement

All acupuncturists' assistants must be supervised and be employed by or work under the physical direction, control, and supervision of a physician or certified acupuncturist (medical doctor with six months of traditional Chinese acupuncture training) certified by the board to practice acupuncture. The acupuncturists' assistant must perform such duties, services and functions assigned by said employer at a place of employer's practice unless said duties, services, and functions are performed in the physical presence of said employer or licensed physician or certified acupuncturist.

Malpractice Insurance Requirement

Professional liability insurance is not mandated.

Health Insurance Coverage

Neither third party reimbursement nor reimbursement under workers' compensation is mandated.

Practice of Acupuncture by Other Healthcare Providers

Information Provided by the State Board of Medical Examiners in 2000: A medical doctor or osteopath may be certified as an acupuncturist if she or he has successfully completed six months of training in traditional Chinese acupuncture in a school or clinic approved by the board.

Neither a podiatrist nor a physician assistant may practice acupuncture within his or her scope of practice.

Information Provided by the Board of Chiropractic Examiners in 2004: A chiropractor wishing to practice acupuncture must comply with the provisions of R.S. 37:1358.

(ed.~same provisions as for acupuncturists' assistants.)

Continuing Education Requirement

None.

Chemical Dependency Specialists

There is no provision for the practice of acupuncture by chemical dependency specialists.

MAINE

Year first statute passed: 1987

Statute #: 32 MRSA, Chapter 113-B

Regulatory Agency Contact:
Ms. Geraldine L. Betts, Administrator
Department of Professional and Financial
Regulation
Office of Licensing and Registration
#35 State House Station
Augusta, ME 04333
(207) 624-8600
(207) 624-8637 FAX
(207) 624-8563 TDD
www.maineprofessionalreg.org

 # Licensed Practitioners: 90

Title of license:
Licensed Acupuncturist

Use of titles:
No information provided.

Fees:

Application		$75
Criminal History Record Check		$15
Initial License		$325
Biennial Renewal		$325

Governing Body

Board of Complementary Health Care Providers. This joint board is composed of two licensed acupuncturists, two members eligible for licensure in naturopathic medicine, one licensed allopathic or osteopathic physician, one licensed pharmacist and one public member.

Definition of Acupuncture

According to statute—*"acupuncture" means the insertion of fine metal needles through the skin at specific points on or near the surface of the body with or without the palpation of specific points on the body and with or without the application of electric current or heat to the needles or skin, or both. The practice of acupuncture is based on traditional Oriental theories and serves to normalize physiological function, treat certain diseases and dysfunctions of the body, prevent or modify the perception of pain and promote health and well-being.*

Effective April, 2004—*the scope of practice of acupuncturists includes acupuncture and the allied techniques and modalities of the distinct system of health care that use Oriental principles to diagnose and treat illness, injury, pain and other conditions by regulating the flow and balance of energy to restore and maintain health. These allied techniques and modalities include the following, as defined by and used exclusively in accordance with the traditions and formal curricula taught in accredited colleges of acupuncture: Oriental diagnostic procedures; electrical and magnetic stimulation; moxibustion and other forms of heat therapy; sound, light and vibrational therapy; cupping techniques and gwa sha; recommendation and dispensing of Chinese patent remedies or Chinese premade herbal remedies and lifestyle and dietary counseling; formulation and dispensing of custom-made Chinese herbal formulations, to the extent that an acupuncturist has received additional certification pursuant to subsection 3; sotai; shiatsu; qi gong; zero balancing; tuina; and acupressure. These techniques and modalities do not include manipulation or mobilization of the skeletal articulations of the human body.*

Eligibility Requirements for Licensure

Formal Education Requirements: A minimum of 1,000 hours of classroom instruction in acupuncture and related subjects at an institution approved by the board and a minimum of 300 hours of clinical experience in the field of acupuncture.

Undergraduate Requirements: Baccalaureate degree from an accredited institution of higher learning, a license from the state to practice as a registered professional nurse, or successful completion of the training program and any competency examination required by the Board of Licensure in Medicine to be qualified as a physician assistant.

Apprenticeship: Not a route of eligibility.

Written Exam: The NCCAOM examination in English is required.

Practical Exam: None specified.

Other Eligibility Requirements: Effective April, 2004, certification is required for licensed acupuncturists to practice the formulation and dispensing of custom-made Chinese herbal formulations. The board shall adopt rules specifying the training required for licensed acupuncturists to obtain the certification for custom-made Chinese herbal formulation.

Reciprocity/Endorsement: Endorsement for acupuncture licensing is possible with a current, valid license to practice acupuncture from another state which has requirements at least equal to Maine's requirements.

Practice of Acupuncture by Other Healthcare Providers

A person may not practice acupuncture unless that person holds a current and valid license, with the exception that this does not apply to any person who is licensed to practice any healing art or science and who is practicing acupuncture in the course of that practice and within the scope of that license.

Information Provided by the Board of Licensure in Medicine in 2004: Acupuncture is within the scope of practice of medical doctors. No specific training requirements have been set.

A physician assistant may use acupuncture if the supervising physician is competent in acupuncture, or if the physician assistant has access to such competence, and the supervising physician has delegated the authority to perform acupuncture.

Information Provided by the Board of Chiropractic Examiners in 2004: Chiropractors must complete a board approved 200-hour course in "chiropractic acupuncture." The course must include supervised clinical training, clean needle technique training and written and practical verification of competency. Chiropractic acupuncture is limited to those methods and procedures that are commonly taught by accredited chiropractic col-

Practice of Acupuncture by Other Healthcare Providers, continued

leges and have been approved by the board. D.C.s practicing chiropractic acupuncture must be trained in blood borne pathogens and register as a biomedical waste generator with the Department of Environmental Protection. Twelve hours of continuing education are required every two years.

Information Provided by the Board of Complementary Health Care Providers in 2004: Regarding the practice of acupuncture by naturopathic doctors: "Naturopathic acupuncture" means the insertion of acupuncture needles into specific points on the skin to treat human disease and impairment and to relieve pain. The practice of naturopathic acupuncture is only within the scope of practice of specialty certified naturopathic doctors.

The board may issue a specialty certification in acupuncture to a licensed naturopathic doctor who has completed an acupuncture program approved by the board that includes 1,000 hours of classroom training and 300 hours of supervised clinical training and passed an examination administered by the NCCAOM.

A licensee must have an additional 15 hours of board approved continuing education annually, specific to acupuncture.

MAINE

Supervision or Referral Requirement

None.

Continuing Education Requirement

Upon biennial renewal: 30 continuing education units. Continuing education credit will be given for programs which are directly related to the knowledge and clinical practice of acupuncture and Oriental medicine.

Malpractice Insurance Requirement

Professional liability insurance is not mandated.

Health Insurance Coverage

All individual and group insurance policies providing coverage for acupuncture must provide coverage for those services when performed by a licensed acupuncturist under the same conditions that apply to the services of a licensed physician. (Title 24-A, section 2837-B and section 2745-B.)

Chemical Dependency Specialists

There is no provision for the practice of acupuncture by chemical dependency specialists.

Notes

Please refer to the Board of Complementary Health Care Providers practice act at www.maineprofessional-reg.org for details on current laws, rules, and application packets. Public Law 2004 Chapter 666, enacted by the Maine Legislature on April 26, 2004, amended the scope of practice for acupuncturists and created a new certification level for licensed acupuncturists who practice Chinese herbal formulations.

MARYLAND

Year first statute passed: 1973

Statute #: 1A-101-502

Regulatory Agency Contact:
Ms. Penny Heisler
Maryland Board of Acupuncture
Room 321
4201 Patterson Avenue
Baltimore, MD 21215
(410) 764-4766 / (800) 530-2481
(410) 358-7258 FAX
www.dhmh.state.md.us/bacc

Fees: Initial License $450
         Biennial Renewal $525

 # Licensed Practitioners: 740

Title of license:
Licensed Acupuncturist

Use of titles:
An acupuncturist must identify him or herself as a "licensed acupuncturist" while doing treatment and may not use the word "doctor" unless he or she is licensed as a physician. Unless authorized to practice acupuncture under the acupuncture statute, a person may not use the words or terms "acupuncturist," "licensed acupuncturist," "L.Ac.," or any other words, letters, or symbols with the intent to represent that the person is authorized to practice acupuncture.

Governing Body

The Maryland Board of Acupuncture is composed of seven members appointed by the Governor; five are licensed acupuncturists and two are consumer members.

Definition of Acupuncture

According to statute—*acupuncture means a form of healthcare, based on a theory of energetic physiology, that describes the interrelationship of the animal or human body organs or functions with an associated point or combination of points. Practice acupuncture means the use of Oriental medical therapies for the purpose of normalizing energetic physiological functions including pain control, and for the promotion, maintenance, and restoration of health. Practice acupuncture includes 1) stimulation of points of the body by the insertion of acupuncture needles; 2) the application of moxibustion; and, 3) manual, mechanical, thermal, or electrical therapies only when performed in accordance with the principles of Oriental acupuncture medical theories.*

The treatment of animals is within the scope of practice. 135 hours of training in animal acupuncture are required.

Homeopathy is not within the scope of practice of acupuncture.

Eligibility Requirements for Licensure

Formal Education Requirements: The statute requires that an applicant shall have graduated from a course of training of at least 1,800 hours, including 300 clinical hours, that is approved by the Maryland Higher Education Commission, approved by ACAOM or found by the board to be equivalent to a course approved by ACAOM. An applicant need not take an examination if she or he has met these educational qualifications.

Undergraduate Requirements: None specified.

Apprenticeship: Not a route of eligibility.

Experience: Not a route of eligibility.

Other Eligibility Requirements: An applicant must demonstrate proof of proficiency in the written and oral communication of the English language by providing evidence that he or she has completed at least 60 credits from an English-speaking undergraduate or professional school; achieved a passing score on the TOEFL within the previous two years, and a score of at least 180 on the TSE; or passed the NCCAOM or equivalent exam in English and has achieved a passing score of 180 on the TSE.

Written Exam: Passage of the NCCAOM examination and certification as a diplomate in acupuncture. No other education or training need be documented. The NCCAOM examination is not required for applicants who meet the educational requirements.

Practical Exam: None specified.

NCCAOM Credentials Documentation Review Accepted: No.

Reciprocity/Endorsement: No.

Supervision or Referral Requirement

None.

Malpractice Insurance Requirement

Professional liability insurance is not mandated.

Health Insurance Coverage

Neither third party reimbursement nor reimbursement under workers' compensation is mandated.

Chemical Dependency Specialists

An "auricular detoxification aide" may practice auricular acupuncture only under the supervision of a licensed acupuncturist approved by the board, in a board-approved clinical setting, upon successful completion of a training program that meets or exceeds NADA standards. The applicant must already be a certified or licensed healthcare professional (see *full rule for list of accepted categories*).

Practice of Acupuncture by Other Healthcare Providers

Dentists and veterinarians may perform acupuncture with regard to dentistry and veterinary medicine without meeting these requirements.

Information Provided by the Board of Physicians in 2000: Medical doctors must complete at least 250 hours of training in acupuncture before they can practice.

Information Provided by the Board of Chiropractic Examiners 2000: Acupuncture is not within the scope of practice of chiropractors.

Continuing Education Requirement

Upon biennial renewal: 40 hours of continuing education. Up to 15 hours in practice management and/ or teaching are accepted. Distance learning is accepted if sponsored by a recognized or accredited organization, or approved by another state.

Notes

There is a provision for practice by students and visiting teachers.

MASSACHUSETTS

Year first statute passed: 1986

Statute #: 589

Regulatory Agency Contact:
Ms. Ann Marie Casey
Board of Registration in Medicine
Committee on Acupuncture
560 Harrison Avenue, Suite G4
Boston, MA 02118
(617) 654-9869
(617) 357-8453 FAX
www.massmedboard.org/acupuncture

Fees: Initial License $150
        Biennial Renewal $100

 # Licensed Practitioners: 941

Title of license:
Licensed Acupuncturist

Use of titles:
A licensee may not represent that she holds a Ph.D., O.M.D., M.A. or other doctoral or masters degree in the field of acupuncture and/or Oriental medicine unless the educational program which awarded the degree is approved by ACAOM or another committee-approved federal accrediting agency to grant doctorate or masters' degrees.

Governing Body

Board of Registration in Medicine. An advisory committee, the Committee on Acupuncture, is composed of one medical doctor from the board, one physician with two years of experience in acupuncture, one lay person and four licensed acupuncturists.

Definition of Acupuncture

According to statute—*acupuncture, the practice of medicine based on traditional oriental medical theories; primarily the insertion of metal needles through the skin at certain points on the body, with or without the use of herbs, with or without the application of electric current, and with or without the application of heat to the needles, skin or both, in an attempt to relieve pain or improve body function. Electroacupuncture, whether utilizing electrodes on the surface of the skin or current applied to inserted needles, and laser acupuncture are considered the practice of acupuncture.*

The rules include gwa sha, acupatches, herbal poultices, ion cord devices, massage, reflexology, shiatsu, tuina, ryodoraku, Kirlian photography, thermography, German electroacupuncture, breathing exercises, oriental nutritional counseling, nonprescription substances which meet FDA guidelines, therapeutic exercises and lifestyle, behavioral and stress counseling.

Treatment of Animals: As of December 1991, the policy of the Committee on Acupuncture is that a person must have an acupuncture license to perform acupuncture on animals and should have a referral from a licensed veterinarian for acupuncture.

Homeopathy is not within the scope of practice of acupuncturists.

Eligibility Requirements for Licensure

Formal Education Requirements: An applicant must have successfully completed two years of training in one or more acupuncture schools; shall have graduated from a Committee on Acupuncture-approved school; must have a minimum of 1,350 clinical and didactic training and 30 hours of Committee on Acupuncture-approved herbal education. An applicant must document 100 hours of clinic with sole responsibility for diagnosis and treatment of patients within the required 1,350 hours of acupuncture education. If the school is in the U.S., District of Columbia, Puerto Rico, or a U.S. territory, it must be accredited by, or in candidacy status with, ACAOM.

Undergraduate Requirements: Two academic years at an accredited university/college, including courses in human anatomy and physiology and general biology.

Apprenticeship: Not a route of eligibility.

Experience: Not a route of eligibility.

NCCAOM Credentials Documentation Review: No.

Other Eligibility Requirements: An applicant must be at least 18 years old, of good moral character and demonstrate sufficient knowledge of the English language so that he or she may be understood...or have a translator available to communicate with patients. Passage of the NCCAOM exam, a clean needle technique course or the Massachusetts oral exam in English gives presumption of competency. The committee requires passage of the TOEFL with a minimum score of 550. An applicant who fails to demonstrate proficiency in English shall provide the committee with the name and address of his or her interpreter.

A licensee who wishes to use herbal therapy, patent or raw herbs, must obtain approval from the Committee on Acupuncture by submitting evidence of (1) completion of a ACAOM accredited or candidate status oriental medicine program; (2) completion of an herbal medicine program offered by a ACAOM accredited or candidate school that meets ACAOM curriculum requirements regarding herbal medicine or (3) completion of an herbal program which the committee deems is substantially equivalent to or exceeds the ACAOM curriculum requirements regarding herbal medicine as described in the ACAOM Accreditation Handbook.

Written Exam: The NCCAOM exam is required.

Practical Exam: The NCCAOM PEPLS and the clean needle technique course offered by CCAOM.

Reciprocity/Endorsement: The rules specify that for reciprocity there must be a reciprocal licensing agreement in effect. None currently exist.

Malpractice Insurance Requirement

Professional liability insurance is not mandated.

Health Insurance Coverage

Neither third party reimbursement nor reimbursement under workers' compensation is mandated.

Supervision or Referral Requirement

None.

Chemical Dependency Specialists

There is no provision for the practice of acupuncture by chemical dependency specialists.

Continuing Education Requirement

Upon biennial renewal: 30 hours of continuing education, 15 of which must be directly related to acupuncture. Western medical or professional activity courses are allowed for the remaining 15 hours. All courses must be approved by the Committee on Acupuncture before they can be applied towards the requirement. Distance learning may be accepted on a case by case basis.

Practice of Acupuncture by Other Healthcare Providers

Licensed physicians and physical therapists are exempted by statute for transcutaneous nerve stimulation.

MASSACHUSETTS

Practice of Acupuncture by Other Healthcare Providers continued...

Information Provided by the Board of Registration in Medicine in 2004: Acupuncture is within the scope of practice for licensed medical doctors and osteopaths. No special training is needed.

Acupuncture is not within the scope of practice of podiatrists or physician assistants.

Practice of Acupuncture by Other Healthcare Providers continued...

Information Provided by the Board of Chiropractic Examiners in 2004: Chiropractors may not practice acupuncture under their chiropractic license.

Notes

There are provisions for temporary licenses for clinical instructors in an approved school, students in an approved postgraduate clinical program or instructors in an approved educational seminar or program demonstrating clinical techniques on patients. Licenses are valid for one year with two renewals maximum. There is provision for inactive status.

An acupuncturist must inform new patients of their right to have disposable needles. Disposable needles must be used for patients with HIV, hepatitis and other blood-borne diseases.

An acupuncturist may not use the word "cure" in any advertisement.

Acupuncture assistants are allowed. They may not diagnose or insert needles but may do cupping, moxibustion, needle removal, gwa sha, and massage of points.

MICHIGAN

Year first statute passed: N/A	**# Licensed Practitioners:** N/A
Statute #: N/A	**Title of license:** N/A
Governing Body: N/A	

There is no practice act for acupuncturists*

Information Provided by the Board of Medicine in 2004

Acupuncture has been determined to be the practice of medicine by the Attorney General. Thus, only medical doctors and osteopaths may practice or supervise acupuncture.

There are no separate training requirements for medical doctors or osteopaths to practice acupuncture other than their medical education and training.

An acupuncturist may practice under the supervision of a medical doctor. A medical doctor or osteopath may supervise an acupuncturist if the medical doctor first examines the patient and determines that acupuncture is the treatment of choice. The medical doctor is responsible for all delegated acts.

Neither a podiatrist nor a physician assistant may practice acupuncture within their scope of practice.

There is no provision for the practice of acupuncture by chemical dependency specialists.

Information Provided by the Board of Chiropractic Examiners in 2004

Acupuncture is not within the scope of practice of a chiropractor.

* Michigan House Bill 5205 providing for the registration of acupuncturists was passed by both houses of the legislature in 2004. However, the legislative session ended in December and the governor had not signed the bill.

MINNESOTA

Statute #: MS 147B

Regulatory Agency Contact:
Ms. Jeanne Hoffman
Board of Medical Practice
University Park Plaza
2829 University Avenue SE, Suite 500
Minneapolis, MN 55414-3246
(612) 617-1230
(612) 617-2166 FAX
www.bmp.state.mn.us

 # Licensed Practitioners: 316

Title of license:
Licensed Acupuncturist

Use of titles:
An acupuncturist may not use the title "physician" or "doctor" unless also licensed as a physician. The title of "licensed acupuncturist," or the initials "L.Ac.," may be used only by acupuncturists, physicians, osteopaths and chiropractors licensed to practice acupuncture in Minnesota.

Fees:		
	Application	$150
	Initial License	$150
	Annual Renewal	$150

Governing Body

Board of Medical Practice. The Acupuncture Advisory Council, under the Board of Medical Practice, consists of seven members - four licensed acupuncture practitioners, one licensed physician or osteopath who also practices acupuncture, one licensed chiropractor who is NCCAOM certified and one public member who has received acupuncture as a primary therapy from an NCCAOM certified acupuncturist.

Definition of Acupuncture

According to statute—*"acupuncture practice" means a comprehensive system of healthcare using Oriental medical theory and its unique methods of diagnosis and treatment. Its treatment techniques include the insertion of acupuncture needles through the skin and the use of other biophysical methods of acupuncture point stimulation, including the use of heat, Oriental massage techniques, electrical stimulation, herbal supplemental therapies, dietary guidelines, breathing techniques, and exercise based on Oriental medical principles.*

Also included: cupping, dermal friction, acupressure and dietary counseling based on traditional Chinese medical principles.

There is no further definition by rule.

The treatment of animals is not within the scope of practice.

Eligibility Requirements for Licensure

Eligibility Requirements: An applicant must have current, active NCCAOM certification in acupuncture.

Reciprocity/Endorsement: The statute provides for reciprocity for individuals who hold a current license or certificate as an acupuncturist from another jurisdiction if the board determines that the standards for certification or licensure in the other jurisdiction meet or exceed the requirements for licensure in Minnesota and a letter is received from that jurisdiction that the acupuncturist is in good standing in that jurisdiction.

MINNESOTA

Supervision or Referral Requirement

None.

Continuing Education Requirement

Upon annual renewal: applicant must provide documentation of current and active NCCAOM certification.

Health Insurance Coverage

Neither third party reimbursement nor reimbursement under workers' compensation is mandated.

Chemical Dependency Specialists

There is no provision for the practice of acupuncture by chemical dependency specialists.

Malpractice Insurance Requirement

Professional liability insurance is not mandated.

Practice of Acupuncture by Other Healthcare Providers

The statute exempts physicians, osteopaths, and chiropractors.

Information Provided by the Board of Medical Practice in 2000: A medical doctor or osteopath may practice acupuncture. There are no specific training requirements.

Information Provided by the State Board of Chiropractic Examiners in 2004: A chiropractor may practice acupuncture upon registration with the board and documentation of 100 hours of training in acupuncture. Those who do not have proof of training may provide an affidavit affirming completion of 100 hours prior to December 31, 1989, and performance of 500 acupuncture patient visits per year for at least three years, and committing to completion of 10 hours of continuing education in acupuncture within six months of registering with the board. They must also pass the examination in acupuncture administered by the National Board of Chiropractic Examiners or the NCCAOM exam in acupuncture. Registration fee - $100. Annual renewal - $50. Sterilization requirements are specified.

Notes

The acupuncturist must obtain informed consent from the patient. The acupuncturist must ask the patient if he or she has been examined by a licensed physician or other professional with regard to the presenting illness or injury, and shall review the diagnosis as reported. An acupuncturist must refer to other healthcare practitioners when the patient has potentially serious disorders including, but not limited to, cardiac conditions including uncontrolled hypertension; acute, severe abdominal pain; acute, undiagnosed neurological changes; unexplained weight loss or gain in excess of 15 percent of the body weight in less than a three month period; suspected fracture or dislocation; suspected systemic infections; any serious undiagnosed hemorrhagic disorder and acute respiratory distress without previous history. The acupuncturist shall request a consultation or written diagnosis from a licensed physician for patients with potentially serious disorders.

MISSISSIPPI

Year first statute passed: N/A	**# Licensed Practitioners:** N/A
Statute #: N/A	**Title of license:** N/A
Governing Body: N/A	

There is no practice act for acupuncturists

Information Provided by the Board of Medicine in 2004

Acupuncture may be performed in the state of Mississippi only by a physician (1) licensed to practice medicine or surgery in the State, and (2) adequately trained in the above subject. Such licensed individuals wishing to utilize acupuncture in their practice may do so provided that any and all portions of the acupuncture treatment are performed by the person so licensed and no surrogate is authorized in this state to serve in his or her stead. The practice of acupuncture should follow the same quality of standard that the physician, or any other physician in his community, would render in delivering any other medical treatment. Adopted January 20, 2000.

There is no provision for the practice of acupuncture by chemical dependency specialists.

Information Provided by the Board of Chiropractic Examiners in 2004

A chiropractor may not practice acupuncture. Chiropractors can not puncture the skin or enter any body orifices.

MISSOURI

Year first statute passed: 1998

Statute #: 324.475–324.499 RSMO

Regulatory Agency Contact:
Ms. Loree Kessler
Acupuncturist Advisory Committee
PO Box 1335
Jefferson City, MO 65102-1335
(573) 526-1555
(573) 751-0735 FAX
http://pr.mo.gov

 # Licensed Practitioners: 57

Title of license:
Licensed Acupuncturist

Use of titles:
The title "licensed acupuncturist" is reserved for persons licensed under the acupuncture practice act.

Fees: Initial License $500
        Biennial Renewal $500

Governing Body

Board of Chiropractic Examiners. The Acupuncturist Advisory Committee is composed of five members appointed by the governor with the advice and consent of the senate. It is comprised of three licensed acupuncturists, one chiropractic physician and one member from the State Board of Chiropractic Examiners.

Definition of Acupuncture

According to statute—*"acupuncture," is the use of needles inserted into the body by piercing of the skin and related modalities, for the assessment, evaluation, prevention, treatment, or correction of any abnormal physiology or pain by means of controlling and regulating the flow and balance of energy in the body so as to restore the body to its proper functioning and state of health.*

Eligibility Requirements for Licensure

Eligibility Requirements: an applicant must be (a) actively certified as a diplomate in acupuncture by the National Commission for the Certification of Acupuncture and Oriental Medicine; or (b) actively licensed, certified or registered in a state or jurisdiction of the United States which has eligibility and examination requirements that are at least equivalent to those of the National Commission for the Certification of Acupuncture and Oriental Medicine, as determined by the committee and approved by the board.

Malpractice Insurance Requirement

Professional liability insurance is not mandated.

Health Insurance Coverage

Neither third party reimbursement nor reimbursement under workers' compensation is mandated.

Continuing Education Requirement

Requirements for continuing education upon licensure renewal are the same as those required for renewal of NCCAOM certification. Hours in practice management and distance learning are accepted if accepted by NCCAOM. *See note at end of listing.*

MISSOURI

Supervision or Referral Requirement

None.

Practice of Acupuncture by Other Healthcare Providers

Information Provided by the State Board of Healing Arts in 2004: A medical doctor or osteopath may practice acupuncture without any specific training requirements.

Information Provided by the State Board of Chiropractic Examiners in 2004: A chiropractor may practice acupuncture after documenting 100 hours of training and application to the Board for certification. A chiropractor must document 12 hours of continuing education per year specifically in acupuncture. There are 556 chiropractors certified to practice acupuncture.

Chemical Dependency Specialists

The statute provides that auricular detox treatment, consisting of acupuncture needles inserted into specified points in the outer ear of a person undergoing treatment for drug or alcohol abuse or both drug and alcohol abuse, may be done by an "auricular detox technician." An auricular detox technician is a person trained solely in, and who performs only, auricular detox treatment under the supervision of a licensed acupuncturist, physician, or chiropractor. Such treatment shall take place in a hospital, clinic, or treatment facility which provides comprehensive substance abuse services, including counseling, and maintains all licenses and certification necessary and applicable. An auricular detox technician may not insert acupuncture needles in any other points of the ear or body or use the title "licensed acupuncturist."

Notes

Pending Changes to Regulations for 2005 include:

4CSR 15-2.020 License Renewal, Restoration, & Continuing Education

Language is being added to require CE include universal precautions/infection control and CPR.

4CSR 15-3.010 Standards of Practice

Provides requirements when a licensee discontinues practice in Missouri regarding the disposition of patient records.

4CSR 15-4.020 Supervision of Acupuncturist Trainees

Amends the language to reflect current educational requirements of programs not certified by ACAOM.

MONTANA

Year first statute passed: 1974	**# Licensed Practitioners:** 136
Statute #: 37-13-101 ET. SEQ., Montana Code Annotated	**Title of license:** Certified Acupuncturist

Regulatory Agency Contact:
Ms. Evie Martin
Department of Labor and Industry
Board of Medical Examiners
PO Box 200513
Helena, MT 59620-0513
(406) 841-2364
(406) 841-2343 FAX
www.discoveringmontana.com/dli/bsd

Use of titles:
A person may not purport to practice acupuncture or use the title "acupuncturist" or any similar title unless the person is licensed under the provisions of the acupuncture practice act. An acupuncturist may not use the title "doctor" unless he or she is also licensed as a physician.

Fees: Application and
Initial License $65
Annual Renewal $50

Governing Body

Board of Medical Examiners.

Definition of Acupuncture

According to statute, acupuncture is—*the diagnosis, treatment, or correction of human conditions, ailments, diseases, injuries, or infirmities by means of mechanical, thermal, or electrical stimulation effected by the insertion of solid needles.* The term includes the use of acupressure and the use of Oriental food remedies and herbs.

The treatment of animals is not within the scope of practice.

Whether homeopathy is within the scope of practice of acupuncture has not been determined. It is not the practice of medicine.

Eligibility Requirements for Licensure

Formal Education Requirements: An applicant must be a graduate of an approved school of acupuncture that is approved by the NACSCAOM [now ACAOM] and offers a course of at least 1,000 hours of entry-level training in recognized branches of acupuncture or equivalent curriculum approved by the board.

Undergraduate Requirements: None.

Apprenticeship: Not a route of eligibility.

Experience: Not a route of eligibility.

NCCAOM Credentials Documentation Review Accepted: No.

Other Eligibility Requirements: An applicant must be at least 18 years of age and of good moral character.

MONTANA

Written Exam: NCCAOM written exam.

Practical Exam: None specified.

Reciprocity/Endorsement: No.

Supervision or Referral Requirement

None.

Malpractice Insurance Requirement

Professional liability insurance is not mandated.

Health Insurance Coverage

All private insurers must cover services by a licensed acupuncturist. The services of a licensed acupuncturist may be included in nonprofit plans such as prepaid hospital care. Licensed acupuncturists are also included as primary providers under workers' compensation.

Chemical Dependency Specialists

There is no provision for the practice of acupuncture by chemical dependency specialists.

Continuing Education Requirement

None.

Practice of Acupuncture by Other Healthcare Providers

Information Provided by the Board of Medicine and the Board of Chiropractors in 2004: One statute states that a doctor of medicine, osteopathy, chiropractic, dentistry, or podiatry must meet the same requirements, pass an examination and be licensed as an acupuncturist in order to practice acupuncture. An interpretation by the Montana Attorney General held that if a licensed physician wishes to represent himself or herself as licensed to practice the discipline of acupuncture, the physician must acquire a license to practice acupuncture, but that a physician may, as part of his or her practice of medicine, use solid needles to perform therapeutic modalities without first acquiring a license to practice acupuncture.

NEBRASKA

Year first statute passed: 2001

Statute #: 71-1,344–71-1,350

Regulations: 172 NAC 89

Regulatory Agency Contact:
Ms. Vicki Bumgarner
Nebraska Health and Human Services
Credentialing Division
301 Centennial Mall South
PO Box 94986
Lincoln, NE 68509-4986
(402) 471-4911
(402) 471-3577 FAX
(402) 471-9570 TDD
www.state.ne.us

 # Licensed Practitioners: 11

Title of license:
Licensed Acupuncturist

Use of titles:
"Doctor" only with earned doctorate degree.

Fees: Application and
Initial License $301
Biennial Renewal $202

Governing Body

Board of Medicine and Surgery.

Definition of Acupuncture

According to statute—*acupuncture means the insertion, manipulation, and removal of acupuncture needles and the application of manual, mechanical, thermal, electrical, and electromagnetic treatment to such needles at specific points or meridians on the human body in an effort to promote, maintain, and restore health and for the treatment of disease, based on acupuncture theory. Acupuncture may include the recommendation of therapeutic exercises, dietary guidelines, and nutritional support to promote the effectiveness of the acupuncture treatment. Acupuncture does not include manipulation or mobilization or, or adjustment to, the spine, extraspinal manipulation, or the practice of medical nutritional therapy.*

Treatment of animals is not within the scope of practice.

Homeopathy is not within the scope of practice.

Eligibility Requirements for Licensure

Formal Education Requirements: Graduation from a full-time acupuncture program at a university, college or school of acupuncture which includes at least 1,725 hours of entry-level acupuncture education consisting of a minimum of 1,000 didactic and 500 clinical hours, and is accredited or a candidate for accreditation by ACAOM or is accredited by another accrediting body that is recognized as such by the U.S. Department of Education.

Undergraduate Requirements: None.

Apprenticeship: Not a route of eligibility.

Experience: Not a route of eligibility.

NEBRASKA

NCCAOM Credentials Documentation Review Accepted: No.

Other Eligibility Requirements: Completion of a clean needle technique course approved by the NCCAOM.

Written Exam: NCCAOM written exam in acupuncture.

Practical Exam: NCCAOM PEPLS.

Reciprocity/Endorsement: No.

Supervision or Referral Requirement

The patient must present the acupuncturist with a letter of referral from, or a medical diagnosis and evaluation completed by, a practitioner licensed to practice medicine or osteopathic medicine within ninety days immediately preceding the initial acupuncture treatment.

Malpractice Insurance Requirement

Professional liability insurance is not mandated.

Chemical Dependency Specialists

There is no provision for the practice of acupuncture by chemical dependency specialists.

Continuing Education Requirement

Upon biennial renewal: 50 hours of continuing education and current, active NCCAOM certification.

Practice of Acupuncture by Other Healthcare Providers

Information provided by Nebraska Health and Human Services Credentialing Division in 2004: Acupuncture is within the scope of practice of licensed medical doctors and osteopaths. No training in acupuncture is specified.

Acupuncture is not within the scope of practice of a podiatrist or a physician assistant.

Information provided by the Board of Chiropractic in 2004: Per opinion of the attorney general in 1999, acupuncture may be performed by chiropractors. In addition, acupuncture is specifically included in Section 71-182 of a statute regulating chiropractic which passed in September 2001.

Health Insurance Coverage

Neither third party reimbursement nor reimbursement under workers' compensation is mandated.

Notes

No provisions exist for practitioners practicing acupuncture prior to regulation.

Practitioner must obtain signed informed consent from patient.

NEVADA

Year first statute passed: 1973

Statute #: Nevada Revised Statutes 634A

Regulatory Agency Contact:
Ms. Amy Richards
Nevada State Board of Oriental Medicine
9775 S Maryland Parkway, Suite F-280
Las Vegas, NV 89123
(702) 837-8921
(702) 914-8921 FAX
www.oriental_medicine.state.nv.us

 # Licensed Practitioners: 43

Title of license:
Doctor of Oriental Medicine

Use of titles:
The title of "doctor" is allowed by statute for individuals who are licensed as doctors of Oriental medicine.

Fees:

Application and Initial License		$400
Background Investigation		$300
Annual Renewal		$500

Governing Body

The Nevada State Board of Oriental Medicine consists of five members: Three practitioner members, one medical doctor, and one public member.

Definition of Oriental Medicine

According to statute—*"Oriental medicine" means that system of the healing arts which places the chief emphasis on the flow and balance of energy in the body mechanism as being the most important single factor in maintaining the well-being of the organism in health and disease.* The definition includes the practice of acupuncture and herbal medicine and other services approved by the board.

Eligibility Requirements for Licensure

Formal Education Requirements: Completion of an accredited four-year program of study, or its equivalent, in Oriental medicine at a school or college of Oriental medicine which is approved by the board that includes completion of at least 2,800 hours of instruction, including not less than 2,500 didactic hours, for a student to have graduated before November 25, 2002; or completion of at least 3,000 hours of instruction, including not less than 2,500 didactic hours, for a student to graduate on or after November 25, 2002. The program of study must include training or instruction in the subjects of acupuncture, moxibustion, herbology, Oriental physiology, Oriental pathology, Oriental diagnosis, tuina, biology, physics, chemistry, biochemistry, anatomy, Western physiology, Western pathology, Western diagnosis, pharmacology, laboratory and radiology.

Undergraduate Requirements: Bachelor's degree.

Apprenticeship: Not a route of eligibility.

Experience: Not a route of eligibility.

Other Eligibility Requirements: The applicant must submit evidence that he has lawfully practiced Oriental medicine in another state or foreign country for at least four years. Foreign graduates must achieve a score of at least 550 on the TOEFL.

NEVADA

NCCAOM Credentials Documentation Review Accepted: No.

Written Exam: Examinations in acupuncture and Chinese herbology from a national organization approved by the board.

Practical Exam: Nevada administers a state practical examination twice per year that includes questions on acupuncture, herbal medicine, basic medical science, and jurisprudence. The test must be taken in English.

Reciprocity/Endorsement: No.

Supervision or Referral Requirement

None.

Health Insurance Coverage

Third party reimbursement, including workers' compensation, is mandated.

Malpractice Insurance Requirement

Professional liability insurance is not mandated.

Continuing Education Requirement

Upon annual renewal: 10 hours of continuing education approved by the board.

Chemical Dependency Specialists

There is no provision for the practice of acupuncture by chemical dependency specialists.

Practice of Acupuncture by Other Healthcare Providers

An "assistant in acupuncture" is restricted in his or her activities to those procedures which a licensed, supervising Doctor of Oriental Medicine may request him or her to do by a written order. An assistant in acupuncture may not perform any diagnosis of patients or recommend or prescribe any forms of treatment or medication. An assistant in acupuncture may treat patients only under the direct supervision of a Doctor of Oriental Medicine who is on the same premises where the treatment is to be given. Registration as an "assistant in acupuncture" is $500 per year.

Information Provided by the Board of Medical Examiners in 2004: Acupuncture is within the scope of practice of medical doctors. An M.D. can practice acupuncture if he or she has received "adequate training."

Information Provided by the Board of Chiropractic Examiners in 2000: Chiropractors may neither practice nor supervise acupuncture.

Notes

Out-of-state practitioners who wish to present educational seminars in Nevada must apply to the board for a temporary certificate.

NEW HAMPSHIRE

Year first statute passed: 1997	**# Licensed Practitioners:** 78
Statute #: NH RSA 328-G	**Title of license:** Licensed Acupuncturist

Regulatory Agency Contact:
Ms. Ruth Walter, Licensing Clerk
Department of Health and Human Services
Office of Program Support
Board of Acupuncture Licensing
129 Pleasant Street, Brown Building
Concord, NH 03301-3857
(603) 271-0853
(603) 271-5590 FAX
www.dhhs.nh.gov

Title of license:
Licensed Acupuncturist

Use of titles:
Licensed acupuncturists may not use the title "physician" or "doctor" or any physician's or doctor's insignia.

Fees: Initial License $275
        Annual Renewal $225

Governing Body

The Board of Acupuncture Licensing consists of four acupuncturists and one public member appointed by the governor and approved by the Executive Council.

Definition of Acupuncture

According to statute—*"acupuncture" means primarily the insertion of needles through the skin at certain points on the body, with or without the application of electric current and/or heat, for the purpose of promoting health and balance as defined by the principles of Oriental medicine.*

The scope of practice also includes the allied techniques and modalities of Oriental medicine, both traditional and modern; including diagnostic procedures; electrical and magnetic stimulation; moxibustion and other forms of heat therapy; cupping and scraping techniques; dietary, nutritional, and herbal therapies; lifestyle counseling; acupressure; and massage.

Whether the treatment of animals is within the scope of practice has not been determined.

Homeopathy is within the scope of practice.

Eligibility Requirements for Licensure

Formal Education Requirements: Completion of a postsecondary acupuncture college program that is ACAOM or board approved. All applicants that have graduated from a non-ACAOM college or apprenticeship program must show proof of successful completion of a college level course in anatomy and physiology, be currently licensed in another state, and meet other criteria of clinical training and didactic instruction and/or prove years of patient treatment, teaching, supervising clinic, or publishing.

Undergraduate requirements: An applicant must have a baccalaureate, registered nurse or physician assistant degree from an accredited institution. An applicant who possesses a current, valid license to practice acupuncture from another state who meets all other requirements of licensure may have this requirement waived by the board if certain, specific criteria are met.

Apprenticeship: Applications for apprenticeship will be reviewed on a case by case basis. Apprenticeship programs must demonstrate a balanced approach of clinical training and didactic instruction that parallels the ACAOM core curriculum and that conforms to NCCAOM standards.

Experience: May satisfy one of the criteria needed in the Waiver of the Standard Acupuncture Education Requirement.

NCCAOM Credentials Documentation Review Accepted: Current, active NCCAOM certification through examination, or Credentials Documentation Review is required plus completion of a clean needle technique course approved by the NCCAOM.

Other Eligibility Requirements: The applicant must be 21 years of age or older and of good moral character.

Written Examination: Current, active NCCAOM certification through examination or Credentials Documentation Review is required plus completion of a clean needle technique course approved by the NCCAOM.

Practical Examination: NCCAOM PEPLS.

Reciprocity/Endorsement: No.

Supervision or Referral Requirement

None.

Practice of Acupuncture by Other Healthcare Providers

No person may practice acupuncture without first obtaining a license from the board except physicians licensed under RSA 329 and doctors of naturopathic medicine certified under RSA 328-E:12. Other licensed health care professionals may not hold themselves out to be licensed acupuncturists unless they are licensed under the acupuncture practice act.

Information Provided by the State Board of Medicine in 2000: There is no specific training required for a medical doctor or osteopath to practice acupuncture.

Information Provided by the State Board of Chiropractic Examiners in 2004: According to the State Board of Chiropractic Examiners, chiropractors who complete coursework in acupuncture as part of their degree curriculum for chiropractic may practice acupuncture within the scope of chiropractic practice.

The **Board of Acupuncture Licensing** reported that doctors of chiropractic may insert solid needles as "adjunctive" therapy, but may not call it "acupuncture" or call themselves "acupuncturists. A chiropractor may be exempted from the requirements of the acupuncture licensing statute by the

Practice of Acupuncture by Other Healthcare Providers

Acupuncture Licensing Board if specific requirements are met, including NCCAOM certification in acupuncture. The board reports that, to date, no New Hampshire chiropractors have applied for exemption.

Chemical Dependency Specialists

There is no provision for the practice of acupuncture by chemical dependency specialists.

Malpractice Insurance Requirement

Professional liability insurance is not mandated.

Health Insurance Coverage

Neither third party reimbursement nor reimbursement under workers' compensation is mandated.

Continuing Education Requirement

Upon biennial renewal: 30 hours of continuing education, or current, active NCCAOM certification. Excess CEUs may be carried over into the following biennium. Hours in practice management are not accepted. Distance learning is accepted.

NEW JERSEY

Year first statute passed: 1983

Statute #: N.J.S.A. 45: 2C-1–45:2C-18

Regulatory Agency Contact:
Ms. Terri Goldberg
Division of Consumer Affairs
Board of Medical Examiners
Acupuncture Examining Board
124 Halsey Street, 6th Floor
Newark, NJ 07102
(973) 273-8092
(973) 273-8075 FAX
www.state.nj.us/lps/ca/medical.htm

Fees: Application $50
Examination Fee $225
Biennial Renewal $230

 # Licensed Practitioners: 367

Title of license:
Certified Acupuncturist

Use of titles:
The New Jersey Department of Education statute, and its implementing regulations, prohibit a person from appending degree designations to his or her name unless the degree was earned at an institution meeting the accreditation or recognition criteria set forth in those laws. Someone who has earned an O.M.D. or Ph.D. at an out-of-state institution, which does not meet the regional or national accreditation criteria of the law, may not hold him or herself out as having an O.M.D. or Ph.D.

Governing Body

Board of Medical Examiners. The Acupuncture Examining Board is under the supervision of the Board of Medical Examiners and consists of nine members: four acupuncturists, two medical doctors with two years of experience in acupuncture, two public members and one state representative.

Definition of Acupuncture

According to the statute—*acupuncture means the stimulation of a certain point or points on or near the surface of the body by the insertion of needles to prevent or modify the perception of pain or to normalize physiological functions, including pain control, for the treatment of certain diseases, or dysfunctions of the body and includes the techniques of electroacupuncture, mechanical stimulation and moxibustion.*

The rules include cupping, thermal methods, herbal applications, magnetic stimulation, gwa-sha acupatches, acuform, pressure needles, acutotement, acupressure, laser biostimulation in accordance with relevant federal law, ultrasonic stimulation of acupuncture points and channels, and various types of acupuncture needles. Staples and hypodermic needles are prohibited.

The treatment of animals is not within the scope of practice.

Homeopathy is not within the scope of practice of acupuncture.

Eligibility Requirements for Licensure

Formal Education Requirements: Completion of a board-approved two-year course of study or a board-approved two-year program in a school of acupuncture. Completion of two years of a three- or four-year program is not acceptable; graduation is required.

Undergraduate Requirements: A baccalaureate degree is required for all applicants who apply for licensure based on schooling.

NEW JERSEY

Apprenticeship: An applicant must show successful completion of a board-approved tutorial program of no less than two nor more than four calendar years. The program must be in New Jersey and the preceptor must have seven years experience prior to the beginning of the apprenticeship.

Experience: Applicants for licensure through experience must document three years of experience practicing acupuncture prior to January 18, 1986. The practice must consist of at least 750 patient treatments during each twelve-month period.

NCCAOM Credentials Documentation Review Accepted: No.

Other Eligibility Requirements: An applicant must be 21 years of age and of good moral character. A candidate who received his or her undergraduate degree from a non-English speaking country or a country wherein the language is other than English shall submit a TSE with a minimum score of 50 or its equivalent taken within the previous five years.

Written Exam: The NCCAOM exam in English.

Practical Exam: The NCCAOM PEPLS and the New Jersey state licensure exam.

Licensure by Endorsement: No.

Supervision or Referral Requirement

Initial acupuncture treatment shall only be performed on presentation by the patient of a referral by or diagnosis from a licensed physician. A diagnosis and preevaluation of the patient shall be made available to the treating acupuncturist by the referring or diagnosing physician. In each case, an accurate and detailed clinical record shall be kept by the acupuncturist, which shall include the referring physicians preevaluation of the patient.

Continuing Education Requirement

Upon biennial renewal: 20 hours of continuing education. Hours in practice management are accepted. Distance learning is accepted on a case by case basis.

Health Insurance Coverage

Neither third party reimbursement nor reimbursement under workers' compensation is mandated.

Malpractice Insurance Requirement

Professional liability insurance is not mandated.

Practice of Acupuncture by Other Healthcare Providers

A licensed physician and surgeon or dentist may practice acupuncture provided his or her course of training has included acupuncture. However, no healthcare providers may call themselves "acupuncturists" or "certified acupuncturists" unless they have met the same standards and passed the same examinations as certified acupuncturists.

Information Provided by the New Jersey Acupuncture Examining Board in 2004: In order to practice acupuncture, a medical doctor or osteopath must have 300 hours of training including 150 hours of clinical training approved by the board.

Acupuncture is not within the scope of practice of podiatrists or physician assistants.

Information Provided by the State Board of Chiropractic Examiners in 2004: The practice of acupuncture is not within the scope of practice of chiropractors.

Chemical Dependency Specialists

There is no provision for the practice of acupuncture by chemical dependency specialists.

NEW MEXICO

Year first statute passed: 1981

Statute #: SECTION 61-14A-1 ET SEQ., NMSA, 1978, As Amended

Regulatory Agency Contact:
Ms. Rosemarie Ortiz
New Mexico Board of Acupuncture and Oriental Medicine
PO Box 25101
Santa Fe, NM 87504
(505) 476-4630
(505) 476-4545 FAX
www.rld.state.nm.us

 # Licensed Practitioners: 533

Title of license:
Doctor of Oriental Medicine

Use of titles:
Licensees must use the title "Doctor of Oriental Medicine" or "D.O.M." Effective July 1, 1994, the title Doctor of Oriental Medicine shall supersede the use of all titles that include the words "medical doctor" or the initials "M.D." unless the person is a licensed medical doctor.

Fees:		
	Examination Fee	$450
	Initial License	$500
	Annual Renewal	$200

Governing Body

The Board of Acupuncture and Oriental Medicine, an independent policy making board, is composed of seven individuals: four licensed doctors of oriental medicine and three public members, all appointed by the governor with terms.

Definition of Acupuncture

According to statute—*"acupuncture" means the surgical use of needles inserted into and removed from the body and the use of other devices, modalities and procedures at specific locations on the body for the prevention, cure, or correction of any disease, illness, injury, pain, or other condition by controlling and regulating the flow and balance of energy and function to restore and maintain health. "Oriental medicine" means the distinct system of primary healthcare that uses all allied techniques of Oriental medicine, both traditional and modern, to diagnose, treat and prescribe for the prevention, cure or correction of any disease, illness, injury, pain or other physical or mental condition by controlling and regulating the flow and balance of energy and function to restore and maintain health. "Techniques of Oriental medicine" include but are not limited to moxibustion, herbology, dietary and nutritional counseling, bodywork and breathing and exercise techniques.*

The rules specify an extensive list of accepted treatment modalities and services.

Homeopathy is within the scope of practice.

Postgraduate education defined by the board allows for Extended and Expanded Prescriptive Authority.

Eligibility Requirements for Licensure

Formal Education Requirements: Completion of the following educational program: 2,400 clock hours of classes including a minimum of 1,100 hours of didactic education in acupuncture and Oriental medicine to include 450 didactic herbology hours and a minimum of 900 hours of supervised clinical practice with 400 hours of actual treatment by the student.

Undergraduate Requirements: None

Apprenticeship: All applicants must have completed a minimum of 2,400 hours of training.

Experience: Not a route of eligibility.

NCCAOM Credentials Documentation Review Accepted: No.

Other Eligibility Requirements: An applicant must be of good moral character.

Written Exam: The written examinations approved by the board shall be: (1) the NCCAOM Foundations of Oriental Medicine module; and (2) the NCCAOM Acupuncture module; and (3) the NCCAOM Chinese Herbology module; and (4) the NCCAOM Biomedicine module; and (5) the NCCAOM approved clean needle technique course; and (6) the board approved and board administered jurisprudence examination covering the act and the rules.

Practical Exam: The practical examinations approved by the board shall be: (1) the NCCAOM Point Location module; and (2) the Clinical Skills Examination.

Reciprocity/Endorsement: Regulations are currently being adopted for "Licensure by Endorsement" for implementation in 2005 (Part 17 of the board's rules).

Continuing Education Requirement

The entry level Doctor of Oriental Medicine must provide proof of continuing NCCAOM recertification in Oriental medicine, acupuncture or Chinese herbology; or proof of completion of 15 hours annually of NCCAOM equivalent continuing education courses approved by the board.

Those Doctors of Oriental Medicine that are licensed at the Extended or Expanded Prescriptive Authority level must provide an additional 7 hours of continuing education in areas relating to new substances or updated information about current substances in the prescriptive authority formulary defined in 16.2.2.13 NM (Section 13 of Part 2 of the rules) and in improving current techniques or new or advanced techniques that are part of the extended or expanded prescriptive authority certification approved by the board.

Health Insurance Coverage

The insurance statute contains a statement regarding a patient's freedom of choice in the selection of hospitals or practitioners of the healing arts. Acupuncture practitioners may not be excluded from health maintenance organizations. However, there is no statute or rule that mandates reimbursement for acupuncture treatment.

Practice of Acupuncture by Other Healthcare Providers

Healthcare providers shall not hold themselves out to the public or any private group or business by any title or description of services which includes the term acupuncture, acupuncturist, or doctor of Oriental medicine unless they are licensed under the Acupuncture and Oriental Medicine Practice Act.

Information provided by the Board of Medical Examiners in 2004: Acupuncture is within the scope of practice of medical doctors. Appropriate training is recommended. Acupuncture may be within the scope of practice of physician assistants, provided that medical services delegated to a physician assistant by the supervising physician must be within the scope of the physician assistant's skills and training, form an usual component of the physician's scope of practice, and are rendered under the direction of a board-approved, licensed supervising physician.

Information Provided by the Board of Chiropractic Examiners in 2004: Chiropractors may practice acupuncture but call it meridian therapy. They may not call themselves or promote themselves in the media as acupuncturists. A chiropractor may not supervise an acupuncturist. Rules regarding the practice of acupuncture by chiropractors are under review in January 2005. Contact the Board of Chiropractic Examiners for details.

NEW MEXICO

Chemical Dependency Specialists

The Board is adopting a provision for practice by Certified Auricular Detoxification Specialists (CADS) for implementation in 2005 (Part 16 of the Board's Rules).

Supervision or Referral Requirement

None.

Malpractice Insurance Requirement

Professional liability insurance is not mandated.

NEW YORK

Year first statute passed: 1991

Statute #: Education Law, Article 160, Sections: 8210-8216

Regulatory Agency Contact:
Ms. Ronnie Hausheer
New York Board for Acupuncture
Education Building, 2W
89 Washington Avenue
Albany, NY 12234
(518) 474-3817 Ext. 100
(518) 486-4846 FAX
www.op.nysed.gov/acupun.htm

 # Licensed Practitioners: 2,400+

Title of license:
Licensed Acupuncturist

Use of titles:
The use of the title "doctor" is not legal unless an individual has earned a doctorate degree from a recognized college or university.

Fees: Initial License $750
Triennial Renewal $250

Governing Body

New York State Board of Regents. The state Board for Acupuncture is an advisory board and consists of not less than eleven members: four licensed acupuncturists, four licensed physicians certified to practice acupuncture and three public members. The board advises the Education Department and the Board of Regents.

Definition of Acupuncture

According to statute—*the profession of acupuncture is the treating, by means of mechanical, thermal or electrical stimulation effected by the insertion of needles or by the application of heat, pressure or electrical stimulation at a point or combination of points on the surface of the body predetermined on the basis of the theory of physiological interrelationship of body organs with an associated point or combination of points for diseases, disorders and dysfunctions of the body for the purpose of achieving a therapeutic or prophylactic effect.*

The treatment of animals is not within the scope of practice.

Homeopathy is not within the scope of practice of acupuncture. It is considered to be the practice of medicine.

Eligibility Requirements for Licensure

Formal Education Requirements: Completion of 4,050 clock hours (equivalent to a three-year program) of didactic and clinical work. Completion of an ACAOM accredited program may be accepted as meeting New York's professional education requirement.

Undergraduate Requirements: 60 semester hours of undergraduate work including 9 semester hours of biosciences.

Apprenticeship: Not a route of eligibility.

Experience: Not a route of eligibility.

NCCAOM Credentials Documentation Review Accepted: No.

NEW YORK

Other Eligibility Requirements: An applicant must be 21 years old and of good moral character. Applicants whose application is based upon credit granted for the completion of courses of study in a country where English is not the principal language spoken must demonstrate English language competency. The requirement may be met by taking the NCCAOM exam in English; the General Education Development Test given for the GED Certificate; a proficiency exam taken to meet immigration or licensure requirements such as the Educational Commission for Foreign Medical Graduates, the Visa Qualifying Examination, the Foreign Medical Graduate Examination in the Medical Sciences or the Official Michigan English Language Assessment Battery; scoring 500 on the TOEFL or postsecondary study at a university or college that would be accepted toward meeting degree requirements.

Written Exam: The NCCAOM written examination.

Practical Exam: The NCCAOM PEPLS examination and a clean needle technique course approved by NCCAOM.

Licensure by Endorsement: No.

Practice of Acupuncture by Other Healthcare Providers

A person who is validly registered as a "specialist's assistant - acupuncture" may practice under the supervision of a licensed physician in accordance with New York State Education Law.

Information Provided by the State Board of Acupuncture in 2004: Acupuncture is not within the scope of practice of physical therapy.

Information Provided by the State Board for Medicine in 2000: Licensed physicians, osteopaths, and dentists must be certified to practice acupuncture. They are required to document 300 hours of acceptable training in acupuncture.

Acupuncture is not within the scope of practice of podiatrists or physician assistants.

Information Provided by the State Board for Chiropractic in 2004: Acupuncture is not within the scope of practice of chiropractors.

Health Insurance Coverage

Neither third party reimbursement nor reimbursement under workers' compensation is mandated.

Continuing Education Requirement

None.

Supervision or Referral Requirement

None.

Chemical Dependency Specialists

There is an exemption in the law for acupuncture used in the treatment of alcoholism, substance dependency or chemical dependency in a hospital or clinic program that has received the appropriate approval. These services may be provided by someone who has been trained to practice acupuncture for the treatment of alcoholism, substance dependence or chemical dependency through an approved educational program. Such person may work only under the general supervision of a physician or dentist certified to practice acupuncture or an individual licensed to practice acupuncture in New York State.

Malpractice Insurance Requirement

Professional liability insurance is not mandated.

Notes

Licensed acupuncturists must advise each patient as to the importance of consulting with a licensed physician regarding the patient's condition and must keep on file with the patient's records, a form attesting to the patient's notice of such advice.

NORTH CAROLINA

Year first statute passed: 1993

Statute #: Chapter 303 Article 30

Regulatory Agency Contact:
Ms. Paola Ribadeneira
Acupuncture Licensing Board
PO Box 10686
Raleigh, NC 27605
(919) 821-3008
(919) 833-5743 FAX
www.ncalb.state.nc.us

 # Licensed Practitioners: 227

Title of license:
Licensed Acupuncturist

Use of titles:
Licensure as an acupuncturist does not by itself entitle a person to identify oneself as a doctor or physician.

Fees: Application $100
Initial License $500
Biennial Renewal $300

Governing Body

The Acupuncture Licensing Board consists of six members: four licensed acupuncturists, one licensed physician who has completed at least 200 hours in medical acupuncture training and one layperson.

Definition of Acupuncture

According to statute, acupuncture means—*a form of healthcare developed from traditional and modern Chinese medical concepts that employ acupuncture diagnosis and treatment, and adjunctive therapies and diagnostic techniques, for the promotion, maintenance, and restoration of health and the prevention of disease. "Practice of acupuncture" or "practice acupuncture" means—the insertion of acupuncture needles and the application of moxibustion to specific areas of the human body based upon acupuncture diagnosis as a primary mode of therapy. Adjunctive therapies within the scope of acupuncture may include massage, mechanical, thermal, electrical, and electromagnetic treatment and the recommendation of herbs, dietary guidelines, and therapeutic exercise.*

The treatment of animals not within the scope of practice.

Homeopathy is within the scope of practice.

Eligibility Requirements for Licensure

Formal Education Requirements: Successful completion of a three-year postgraduate program at an acupuncture college accredited by, or in candidacy status with ACAOM or, if outside the United States, the California Acupuncture Committee.

Undergraduate Requirements: None specified.

Apprenticeship: Not applicable.

Experience: Not a route of eligibility.

NCCAOM Credentials Documentation Review Accepted: No.

Other Eligibility Requirements: Successful completion of the clean needle technique course offered by the Council of Colleges of Acupuncture and Oriental Medicine (CCAOM).

NORTH CAROLINA

Written Exam: The NCCAOM written examination.

Practical Exam: The NCCAOM PEPLS.

Licensure by Endorsement: No.

Supervision or Referral Requirement

None.

Chemical Dependency Specialists

There is no provision for the practice of acupuncture by chemical dependency specialists.

Continuing Education Requirement

Upon biennial license renewal: 40 hours of continuing education approved by the board. A minimum of 25 contact hours must be relating to the scope of practice of acupuncture as defined in North Carolina. A maximum of 15 contact hours may be in any health service related area. Hours in practice management are not accepted. Distance learning is accepted if sponsored by approved organizations.

Practice of Acupuncture by Other Healthcare Providers

Information from the North Carolina Medical Board in 2004: Acupuncture is within the scope of practice of licensed physicians. Physicians are expected to have sufficient education and training when rendering any form of medical or surgical care.

Information from the Board of Chiropractic in 2000: Acupuncture is within the scope of practice of licensed chiropractors.

Malpractice Insurance Requirement

Professional liability insurance is not mandated.

Health Insurance Coverage

Neither third party reimbursement nor reimbursement under workers' compensation is mandated.

NORTH DAKOTA

Year first statute passed: N/A	**# Licensed Practitioners:** N/A
Statute #: N/A	**Title of license:** N/A
Governing Body: N/A	

There is no practice act for acupuncturists

Information Provided by the Board of Medical Examiners in 2004

The practice of acupuncture has not been recognized by the Legislative Assembly of North Dakota as a distinct healing art, i.e., North Dakota statutes do not provide for the licensure of persons desiring to practice acupuncture. Under existing statutes, the practice of acupuncture would be construed to be the practice of medicine. Any person who, a) holds himself out to the public as being engaged in the diagnosis or treatment of diseases or injuries of human beings, b) suggests, recommends, or prescribes any form of treatment for the intended relief of cure of any physical or mental ailment of any person, with the intention of receiving, directly or indirectly, any fee, gift, or compensation, or, c) maintains an office for the examination or treatment of persons afflicted with disease or injury of the body or mind, is regarded as practicing medicine in accordance with the provisions of Section 43-17-01, NDCC.

The only persons excluded or exempt from the provisions of the forgoing section are dentists, optometrists, chiropractors, and podiatrists when properly licensed, and religious ceremonies as a form of worship, devotion or healing where no drugs or medicines are prescribed and no surgical or physical operations are performed.

It is, therefore, the conclusion of this office that one must be licensed to practice medicine in North Dakota before being able to establish a practice of acupuncture.

The Board of Medical Examiners has no rules or regulations relating to the practice of acupuncture.

There is no provision for the practice of acupuncture by chemical dependency specialists.

Information Provided by the Board of Chiropractic Examiners in 2000

A chiropractor may perform acupuncture after documentation of 100 hours of acupuncture training sponsored by one of the CCE accredited chiropractic colleges. A chiropractor may not supervise a non-physician acupuncturist.

OHIO

Year first statute passed: 2000

Statute #: Chapter 4762, Ohio Revised Code

Regulatory Agency Contact:
Mr. Tom Dilling, J.D., Director
Ohio State Medical Board
77 South High Street, 17th Floor
Columbus, OH 43215-6127
(614) 466-3934
(614) 728-5946 FAX
www.med.ohio.gov

Fees: Initial License $100
        Biennial Renewal $100

 # Licensed Practitioners: 69

Title of license:
Certificate of Registration–Acupuncturist

Use of titles:
A person who holds a certificate of registration as an acupuncturist may use the following titles, initials, or abbreviations, or the equivalent of such titles, initials, or abbreviations, to identify the person as an acupuncturist: "acupuncturist," "registered acupuncturist," "R.Ac.," "Reg.Ac.," "certified acupuncturist," "C.A.," "diplomate of acupuncture (NCCAOM)," "Dipl.Ac. (NCCAOM)," or "national board certified in acupuncture (NCCAOM)." The person shall not use other titles, initials, or abbreviations in conjunction with the person's practice of acupuncture, including the title "doctor."

Governing Body

Medical Board.

Definition of Acupuncture

According to statute—*"acupuncture" means a form of health care performed by the insertion and removal of specialized needles, with or without the application of moxibustion or electrical stimulation, to specific areas of the body.*

Eligibility Requirements for Licensure

An individual must be a current, active NCCAOM diplomate in acupuncture.

Licensure by Endorsement: No.

Continuing Education Requirement

Current Active NCCAOM certification in acupuncture must be maintained.

Malpractice Insurance Requirement

Professional liability insurance is not mandated.

Health Insurance Coverage

Neither third party reimbursement nor reimbursement under workers' compensation is mandated.

Chemical Dependency Specialists

There is no provision for the practice of acupuncture by chemical dependency specialists.

OHIO

Supervision or Referral Requirement

An acupuncturist may perform acupuncture only if the patient has received a physician's written referral or prescription for acupuncture. The acupuncturist must provide reports to the physician on the patient's condition or progress in treatment and comply with the conditions or restrictions on the acupuncturist's course of treatment. The acupuncturist must perform acupuncture under the general supervision of the patient's referring or prescribing physician. General supervision does not require that the acupuncturist and physician practice in the same office. The physician must be personally available for consultation and in a location that under normal circumstances is not more than sixty minutes travel time from the acupuncturist. Consultation may be by phone. Prior to treating a patient, the acupuncturist shall advise the patient that acupuncture is not a substitute for conventional medical diagnosis and treatment.

Practice of Acupuncture by Other Healthcare Providers

Information Provided by the Medical Board in 2004: Acupuncture is within the scope of practice of a medical doctor without specific training.

Information Provided by the Board of Chiropractic Examiners in 2000: A chiropractor may neither practice nor supervise acupuncture. The chiropractic statute prohibits acupuncture.

OKLAHOMA

Year first statute passed: N/A	**# Licensed Practitioners:** N/A
Statute #: N/A	**Title of license:** N/A
Governing Body: N/A	

There is no practice act for acupuncturists

Information Provided by the Board of Medical Licensure in 2004

No law exists which licenses, regulates, or prohibits acupuncture.

The practice of acupuncture is within the scope of a medical doctor without specific training requirements or registration.

Information Provided by the Board of Chiropractic Examiners in 2004

A chiropractor who practices acupuncture can register with the board. The board accepts and records certification from schools but does not itself certify the practice of acupuncture.

OREGON

Year first statute passed: 1973

Statute #: ORS 677.757–770

Regulatory Agency Contact:
Ms. Diana Dolstra
Board of Medical Examiners
620 Crowne Plaza
1500 SW First Avenue
Portland, OR 97201-5770
(503) 229-5770
(503) 229-6543 FAX
www.bme.state.or.us

 # Licensed Practitioners: 576

Title of license:
Licensed Acupuncturist

Use of titles:
An acupuncturist may not use the title "doctor" or represent him or herself as a physician. Using the term "acupuncture," "acupuncturist," Oriental medicine or any other term, title, name, or abbreviation indicating that an individual is qualified or licensed to practice acupuncture is prima facie evidence of practicing acupuncture.

Fees: Initial License $230
          Annual Renewal $270

Governing Body

Board of Medical Examiners. The Acupuncture Advisory Committee is composed of two licensed physicians, three licensed acupuncturists, and one Board of Medical Examiners member.

Definition of Acupuncture

According to statute—"acupuncture" means an Oriental healthcare practice used to promote health and to treat neurological, organic or functional disorders by the stimulation of specific points on the surface of the body by the insertion of needles. Acupuncture includes the treatment method of moxibustion, as well as the use of electrical, thermal, mechanical or magnetic devices, with or without needles, to stimulate acupuncture points and acupuncture meridians and to induce acupuncture anesthesia or analgesia.

The practice of acupuncture also includes the following modalities as authorized by the Board of Medical Examiners for the State of Oregon: (A) Traditional and modern techniques of diagnosis and evaluation; (B) Oriental massage, exercise and related therapeutic methods; and (C) The use of Oriental pharmacopoeia, vitamins, minerals and dietary advice. "Oriental pharmacopoeia" means a list of herbs described in traditional Oriental texts commonly used in accredited schools of Oriental medicine if the texts are approved by the Board of Medical Examiners for the State of Oregon.

The Board of Medical Examiners issued a memo August 2, 1995 stating that the scope of practice does not include western medical practices, such as laboratory testing and ordering x-rays.

Eligibility Requirements for Licensure

Three Routes of Eligibility

1) Graduation from an acupuncture program that has been granted accreditation or candidacy status by the ACAOM, or from a program evaluated to be equivalent by the Oregon Office of Degree Authorization, as approved by the board, and NCCAOM certification in acupuncture (does not have to be current).

OREGON

2) Experience: (a) Five years of licensed clinical acupuncture practice prior to July 1, 1998, (b) practice as a licensed acupuncturist in the United States during five of the last seven years prior to application, including clinical practice, clinical supervision, teaching, research and other work as approved by the Board within the field of acupuncture and Oriental medicine, (c) current NCCAOM certification and (d) successful completion of the ACAOM western medicine requirements (360 hours) in effect on July 1, 1998.

3) Applicants whose acupuncture training and diploma were obtained in a foreign country and documentation of such cannot be obtained, may be considered eligible for licensure if it is established to the satisfaction of the board that the applicant has equivalent skills and training and can document one year of training or supervised practice under a licensed acupuncturist in the United States.

For All Applicants: (1) A letter of good standing from the states of all prior and current medically related licensure, (2) good moral character, and (3) the ability to communicate in English. The ability to communicate in English is measured if the applicant passed the NCCAOM written examination in English, has passed an English proficiency examination, such as TOEFL or TSE.

Supervision or Referral Requirement

None.

Malpractice Insurance Requirement

Professional liability insurance is not mandated.

Continuing Education Requirement

None.

Chemical Dependency Specialists

There is no provision for the practice of acupuncture by chemical dependency specialists.

Health Insurance Coverage

If an insurance company covers acupuncture performed by a medical doctor, then it must cover acupuncture performed by a licensed acupuncturist.

Acupuncture is covered by workers' compensation within the following guidelines: from date of injury through thirty days an acupuncturist can treat a workers' compensation injury case up to twelve times. However, if the patient sees a medical doctor or chiropractor first, the medical doctor can refer the patient to an acupuncturist but must get approval from the workers' compensation insurance carrier, which has one hundred twenty days to give approval or disapproval.

Practice of Acupuncture by Other Healthcare Providers

Information Provided by the Board of Medical Examiners in 2004: Medical doctors and osteopaths may practice acupuncture without specific training.

Acupuncture is not within the scope of practice of podiatrists or physician assistants.

A physician may not supervise an acupuncturist unless the physician is also a licensed acupuncturist.

Information Provided by the Board of Chiropractic Examiners in 2004: Acupuncture is not within the scope of practice of chiropractic.

Notes

There is limited licensure for visiting professors for one year with a two-year extension possible.

PENNSYLVANIA

Year first statute passed: 1986

Statute #: 63 P.S. 1801-1806 (medical);
63 P.S. 1801-1807 (osteopathic)

Regulatory Agency Contact:
Ms. Gina Bittner
Board of Medicine
Board of Osteopathic Medicine
PO Box 2649
Harrisburg, PA 17105
(717) 783-4858
(717) 783-7769 FAX
www.dos.state.pa.us

 # Licensed Practitioners: 583

Title of license:
Acupuncturist

Use of titles:
An acupuncturist may not use the title "doctor" unless he or she is also a licensed physician.

Fees: Initial License $30
       Biennial Renewal $25

Governing Body

The Board of Medicine and the Board of Osteopathic Medicine. Pennsylvania has two routes of licensure for acupuncturists, one under the medical board and one under the osteopathic board. The provisions of the statutes are the same.

Definition of Acupuncture

According to statute—*acupuncture is the stimulation of certain points on or near the surface of the body by the insertion of needles to prevent or alleviate the perception of pain or to normalize physiological functions, including pain control, for the treatment of certain diseases or dysfunctions of the body. The practice of acupuncture shall also encompass, as regulated by the board, the use of traditional and modern Oriental therapeutics, heat therapy, moxibustion, electrical and low-level laser stimulation, acupressure and other forms of massage, herbal therapy, and counseling that shall include the therapeutic use of foods and supplements and lifestyle modifications and any other techniques approved by the board.*

Eligibility Requirements for Licensure

Formal Education Requirements: Master's degree, master's level certificate or diploma or first professional degree from a degree-granting institution authorized by the Department of Education of the Commonwealth. The degree program must meet or exceed standards required for acupuncture and Oriental medicine programs established by an accrediting agency recognized by the U.S. Department of Education.

Undergraduate Requirements: A person trained in the U.S. must have two years of undergraduate education in addition to acupuncture school.

Apprenticeship: Not a route of eligibility.

Experience: Not a route of eligibility.

NCCAOM Credentials Documentation Review Accepted: Yes, if in 1985-86.

PENNSYLVANIA

Other Eligibility Requirements: There is an English language requirement that may be met by taking the NCCAOM written exam in English or by obtaining a TOEFL of 550.

Written Exam: The NCCAOM exam is required.

Practical Exam: None specified.

Licensure by Endorsement: No.

Supervision or Referral Requirement

A licensed acupuncturist must obtain a written referral and prior diagnosis from a licensed physician, who may place conditions and restrictions on the course of treatment.

Continuing Education Requirement

None.

Chemical Dependency Specialists

There is no provision for the practice of acupuncture by chemical dependency specialists.

Malpractice Insurance Requirement

Professional liability insurance is not mandated.

Health Insurance Coverage

Neither third party reimbursement nor reimbursement under workers' compensation is mandated.

Practice of Acupuncture by Other Healthcare Providers

The statute exempts dentists, podiatrists and veterinarians.

Information Provided by the State Board of Medicine in 2004: Medical doctors must have 200 hours of Category I Continuing Medical Education credits in acupuncture recognized by the Accreditation Council on Continuing Medical Education to be registered as an acupuncturist. All practitioners must register with the board to practice acupuncture.

Information Provided by the State Board of Osteopathic Medicine in 2004: Osteopathic doctors must have 200 hours of Category I Continuing Medical Education credits in acupuncture recognized by the Accreditation Council on Continuing Medical Education to be registered as an acupuncturist. All practitioners must register with the board to practice acupuncture.

Information Provided by the Board of Chiropractic Examiners in 2000: Acupuncture is not within the scope of practice of chiropractors.

Notes

Legislation passed in 2002 changed the requirement for supervision to referral with diagnosis. It also changed educational requirements and expanded the scope of practice to include "supplemental techniques." Rules are still pending.

If a practitioner wishes to receive referrals from both medical doctors and osteopaths, he or she must register with both boards.

RHODE ISLAND

Year first statute passed: 1978

Statute #: RIGL 5-37.2

Regulatory Agency Contact:
Ms. Kelly Doyle
Department of Health and Professional Regulation
Cannon Building
Three Capitol Hill, Room 104
Providence, RI 02908
(401) 222-2828
(401) 222-1272 FAX
www.health.state.ri.us

 # Licensed Practitioners: 131

Title of license:
Doctor of Acupuncture

Use of titles:
"Doctor of acupuncture" is the title of license.

Fees: Application & Initial
License $125
Annual Renewal $312

Governing Body

Department of Health and Professional Regulation.

Definition of Acupuncture

According to statute—*acupuncture means the insertion of needles into the human body by piercing the skin of the body, for the purpose of controlling and regulating the flow and balance of energy in the body.*

The rules do not expand the definition.

The treatment of animals is not within the scope of practice.

Homeopathy is not within the scope of practice.

Eligibility Requirements for Licensure

Formal Education: Graduation from a program approved by ACAOM of at least thirty-six months and not less than 2,500 hours.

Undergraduate Requirements: None specified.

Apprenticeship: Not a route of eligibility.

Experience: Not a route of eligibility.

NCCAOM Credentials Documentation Review Accepted: No.

Other Eligibility Requirements: Applicants must be of good moral character and pass an English proficiency examination.

Written Exam: The NCCAOM exam.

Practical Exam: None specified.

Reciprocity/Endorsement: The state in which the applicant is licensed must meet the same licensing requirements as Rhode Island, have standards as stringent as Rhode Island, and allow reciprocity with Rhode Island.

RHODE ISLAND

Continuing Education Requirement

Upon annual renewal: 20 hours of continuing education. A nationally recognized acupuncture organization or its local chapter or an accredited school of acupuncture must approve the program.

Malpractice Insurance Requirement

Professional liability insurance is not mandated.

Health Insurance Coverage

Neither third party reimbursement nor reimbursement under workers' compensation is mandated.

Chemical Dependency Specialists

There is no provision for the practice of acupuncture by chemical dependency specialists.

Supervision or Referral Requirement

None.

Practice of Acupuncture by Other Healthcare Providers

Information Provided by the Board of Medical Licensure and Discipline in 2000: Medical Doctors may practice medical acupuncture upon completion of a 300-hour course in acupuncture that includes a supervised clinical practicum. Medical doctors must provide patients with disclosure regarding training and that it is not equivalent to the training of licensed Doctors of Acupuncture.

Information Provided by the Board of Chiropractic in 2004: Acupuncture is not within the scope of practice by chiropractors.

SOUTH CAROLINA

Year first statute passed: 1974

Statute #: SC Code Section 40-47-70

Regulatory Agency Contact:
Ms. Annette Disher
Department of Labor and Licensing
Board of Medical Examiners
110 Centerview Drive, Suite 202
PO Box 11289
Columbia, SC 29211-1289
(803) 896-4500
(803) 896-4515 FAX
www.llr.state.sc.us

 # Licensed Practitioners: 47

Title of license:
Acupuncturist

Use of titles:
An acupuncturist may not use the title "doctor" or identify himself or herself as a medical doctor in any way.

Fees: None specified

Governing Body

Board of Medical Examiners. The Acupuncture Committee, and advisory committee, consists of two active Board members, to review applications, examine credentials, interview applicants and act on behalf of the Board to approve applications.

Definition of Acupuncture

There is no definition of acupuncture in statute or regulations.

Eligibility Requirements for Licensure

Formal Education Requirements: None specified

Undergraduate Requirements: None specified.

Apprenticeship: None specified.

Experience: None specified.

NCCAOM Credentials Documentation Review Accepted: No.

Other Eligibility Requirements: An applicant must be NCCAOM certified.

Written Exam: The NCCAOM exam.

Practical Exam: None specified.

Reciprocity/Endorsement: No.

Continuing Education Requirement

Current NCCAOM certification is required for renewal of approval to practice every two years.

Health Insurance Coverage

Neither third party reimbursement nor reimbursement under workers' compensation is mandated.

SOUTH CAROLINA

Supervision or Referral Requirement

Acupuncturists must be referred to, and supervised, by a licensed medical doctor or dentist in facilities approved by the Department of Health and Environmental Control. The supervising physician or dentist must be immediately available to attend to any unexpected, adverse effects. The supervising doctor or dentist shall submit proof of special training in acupuncture or specific knowledge about acupuncture treatments.*

Chemical Dependency Specialists

Individuals who practice auricular acupuncture for drug addiction are exempt from the requirement of NCCAOM certification, but they must be NADA certified.

Malpractice Insurance Requirement

Professional liability insurance is not mandated.

Practice of Acupuncture by Other Healthcare Providers

Information Provided by the State Board of Medical Examiners in 2004: There is no specific coursework required for a medical doctor or osteopath to practice acupuncture.

Podiatrists and physician assistants may not practice acupuncture.

A dentist may practice acupuncture.

Information Provided by the State Board of Chiropractic Examiners in 2004: Acupuncture is not within the scope of practice of a chiropractor. A chiropractor may only practice acupuncture by obtaining permission through the South Carolina Board of Medical Examiners.

Notes

*The South Carolina General Assembly passed a bill (H3891) in June of 2004 that would have, in addition to other changes, removed the requirements for supervision and referral. The bill was vetoed by the governor on December 15, 2004. As this book was going to press, the governor's veto had been overridden by the House. Please contact the state agency for the current status of this legislation.

SOUTH DAKOTA

Year first statute passed: N/A	**# Licensed Practitioners:** N/A
Statute #: N/A	**Title of license:** N/A
Governing Body: N/A	

There is no practice act for acupuncturists

Information Provided by the Board of Medical and Osteopathic Examiners in 2004

There is no statute regulating acupuncture in South Dakota. The issue of whether acupuncture is the practice of medicine or is within the scope of practice of medical doctors and osteopaths has not been determined.

There is no provision for the practice of acupuncture by chemical dependency specialists.

Information Provided by the Board of Chiropractic Examiners in 2000

Acupuncture has been ruled by the Attorney General to be within the scope of practice of chiropractors under the section allowing venipuncture for diagnostic purposes. The board has adopted a policy requiring 100 hours of coursework, passage of the board exam on acupuncture and documentation of an additional 100 hours of education within two years.

TENNESSEE

Year first statute passed: 2000

Statute #: Title 4 Chapter 29

Regulatory Agency Contact:
Ms. Marsha Arnold
Advisory Committee for Acupuncture
Cordell Hull Building, 1st Floor
425 Fifth Avenue North
Nashville, TN 37247-1010
(615) 532-4384
(615) 253-4484 FAX
www.state.tn.us/health

 # Licensed Practitioners: 69

Title of license:
Licensed Acupuncturist

Use of titles:
No person who is not properly licensed to practice medicine shall identify himself or herself as a doctor or physician. Licensed physicians certified by the American Academy of Medical Acupuncture may use the title "acupuncturist."

Fees: Initial License $760
Biennial Renewal $510

Governing Body

Board of Medicine. The Tennessee Advisory Committee for Acupuncture, under the Board of Medicine, consists of three certified acupuncturists, one ADS, and one consumer member.

Definition of Acupuncture

According to statute—*"acupuncture" means a form of healthcare developed from traditional and modern Oriental medical concepts that employs Oriental medical diagnosis and treatment, and adjunctive therapies and diagnostic techniques, for the promotion, maintenance, and restoration of health and the prevention of disease. "Practice of acupuncture" means the insertion of acupuncture needles and the application of moxibustion to specific areas of the human body based upon oriental medical diagnosis as a primary mode of therapy. Adjunctive therapies within the scope of acupuncture may include acupressure, cupping, thermal, and electrical treatment, and the recommendation of dietary guidelines and supplements and therapeutic exercise based on traditional oriental medical concepts.*

The treatment of animals is not within the scope of practice.

Homeopathy is not within the scope of practice of acupuncture.

Eligibility Requirements for Licensure

Formal education requirements: Successful completion of a three-year postsecondary training program or acupuncture college program that is ACAOM accredited or in candidacy status, or which meets ACAOM standards.

Other Eligibility Requirements: Current, active NCCAOM certification as a diplomate in acupuncture and successful completion of a clean needle technique course approved by the NCCAOM.

There is a grandparenting provision for individuals residing in Tennessee on the effective date of the statute and who have completed an approved apprenticeship or tutorial program that meets NCCAOM standards.

Reciprocity/Endorsement: An applicant may be licensed who documents current state licensure in good standing in another state with substantially equivalent or higher standards.

TENNESSEE

Continuing Education Requirement

None.

Supervision or Referral Requirement

None.

Practice of Acupuncture by Other Healthcare Providers

Information Provided by the Medical Board in 2004*: Acupuncture is within the scope of practice of a medical doctor.

Information Provided by the State Board of Chiropractic Examiners in 2004: Acupuncture is not within the scope of practice of chiropractors.

Malpractice Insurance Requirement

Professional liability insurance is not mandated.

Health Insurance Coverage

Neither third party reimbursement nor reimbursement under workers' compensation is mandated.

Chemical Dependency Specialists

According to statute—*"ADS" means an acupuncture detoxification specialist trained in, and who performs only, the five (5) point auricular detoxification treatment.* An ADS must complete a board-approved training program in auricular detoxification acupuncture that meets or exceeds NADA standards, practice auricular detox treatment in a hospital, clinic, or treatment facility that provides comprehensive alcohol and substance abuse or chemical dependency services, including counseling, under the supervision of a licensed acupuncturist or medical director, satisfy all appropriate ethical standards and limit their practice to the five point auricular detoxification treatment. The initial certification fee is $110; biennial renewal is $60.

Notes

Acupuncturists must use disposable needles. The use of staples is prohibited.

*An additional note from the medical board in 2004: the chiropractic board is awaiting the opinion of the attorney general concerning "chiropractic acupuncture."

TEXAS

Year first statute passed: 1993	**# Licensed Practitioners:** 627
Statute #: Texas Revised Civil Statutes Annotated, Article 44956, Subchapter F	**Title of license:** Licensed Acupuncturist
Regulatory Agency Contact: Mr. Tim Speer Board of Medical Examiners PO Box 2018, MC-231 Austin, TX 78768-2018 (512) 305-7067 (512) 305-9416 FAX www.tsbme.state.tx.us	**Use of titles:**

Fees: Initial License $300
Annual Renewal $250

Governing Body

The Board of Medical Examiners is responsible for final approval of licenses, disciplinary actions, and promulgation of rules. The Board of Acupuncture Examiners is an advisory body composed of nine members appointed by the governor, including four acupuncturists, two physicians who are experienced in the practice of acupuncture and three public members.

Definition of Acupuncture

According to statute—*acupuncture means (A) the insertion of an acupuncture needle and the application of moxibustion to specific areas of the human body as a primary mode of therapy to treat and mitigate a human condition; and (B) the administration of thermal or electrical treatments or the recommendation of dietary guidelines, energy flow exercise, or dietary or herbal supplements in conjunction with the treatment described by Paragraph (A) of this subdivision.*

The treatment of animals is not within the scope of practice.

Whether homeopathy is within the scope of practice of acupuncture has not been determined.

Eligibility Requirements for Licensure

Formal Education Requirements: Graduation from a board-approved school of not less than six terms in residence of four months each for a total of not less than 1,800 instructional hours, with at least two terms in residence in supervised patient treatment. The course of study must include anatomy-histology, bacteriology, physiology, symptomatology, pathology, meridian and point locations, hygiene, and public health. The rules require that a school in the United States be ACAOM accredited or in candidacy status and that foreign schools must be substantially equivalent to a ACAOM approved school.

Undergraduate Requirements: An applicant must have completed at least 60 semester hours of college courses, including basic science courses determined by the advisory board.

Apprenticeship: Not determined.

Experience: Not determined.

NCCAOM Credentials Documentation Review Accepted: No.

TEXAS

Other Eligibility Requirements: An applicant must be at least 21 years of age.

All applicants must schedule a personal interview at the offices of the Board of Medical Examiners. Passage of the clean needle technique course offered through the CCAOM is also required.

Written Exam: A applicant must pass the NCCAOM examination in acupuncture as well as the NCCAOM examination in Chinese herbology.

Practical Exam: NCCAOM PEPLS.

Reciprocity/Endorsement: No.

Supervision or Referral Requirement

A patient must be evaluated by a physician or dentist, as appropriate, for the condition being treated by acupuncture within six months before the date acupuncture was first performed. An acupuncturist may treat a patient referred by a licensed chiropractor if the treatment commences within thirty days of the date of referral. Patients receiving acupuncture treatment must be referred to a physician after twenty treatments or thirty days, whichever occurs first, if no substantial improvement occurs in the person's condition for which the referral was made. An acupuncturist may, without referral from a physician, dentist, or chiropractor, perform acupuncture on a person for smoking addiction, weight loss, or, as established by the medical board with advice from the acupuncture board by rule, substance abuse.

Chemical Dependency Specialists

Auricular acupuncture may be provided by a social worker, licensed professional counselor, licensed psychologist, licensed chemical dependency counselor or licensed registered nurse for the purpose of treating alcoholism, substance abuse and chemical dependency if he or she has completed a training program of at least 70 hours, including a clean needle technique course or equivalent universal infection control precaution procedures course approved by the medical board and has been certified by the medical board. The title of certification is "certified acudetox specialist."

Practice of Acupuncture by Other Healthcare Providers

The acupuncture licensing act does not prohibit the practice of acupuncture by a physician.

Information Provided by the Board of Medical Examiners in 1998: The practice of acupuncture is within the scope of practice of medical doctors and osteopaths.

Information Provided by the State Board of Chiropractic Examiners in 2004: A chiropractor may practice acupuncture if he or she is properly trained and practices due diligence.

Continuing Education Requirement

Upon annual renewal: 17 hours of continuing education of which at least 5 hours must be in herbology and at least 2 hours in ethics. Distance learning accepted on a case-by-case basis.

Malpractice Insurance Requirement

Professional liability insurance is not mandated.

Health Insurance Coverage

Neither third party reimbursement nor reimbursement under workers' compensation is mandated.

UTAH

Year first statute passed: 1983	**# Licensed Practitioners:** 64
Statute #: Title 58, Chapter 72	**Title of license:** Licensed Acupuncturist

Regulatory Agency Contact:
Mr. Daniel T. Jones, Bureau Manager
Division of Occupational and Professional
Licensing
160 East 300 South, Box 146741
Salt Lake City, UT 84114-6741
(801) 530-6767
(801) 530-6511
www.dopl.utah.gov

Use of titles:
An acupuncturist may not use the term "physician" or "doctor" in conjunction with his or her name or practice but may use "Doctor of acupuncture" or "Oriental Medical Doctor" if she or he has earned that degree.

Fees:	Initial License	$110
	Biennial Renewal	$63

Governing Body

The Division of Occupational and Professional Licensing. The Board of Acupuncture is and advisory body composed of two acupuncturists, one physician with experience in acupuncture, one other healthcare practitioner with knowledge of and experience in acupuncture, and one member of the general public.

Definition of Acupuncture

According to statute—*"practice of acupuncture" means the insertion of acupuncture needles and application of moxibustion to specific areas of the human body based on traditional Oriental medical diagnosis and concepts as a primary mode of therapy. Adjunctive therapies within the scope of acupuncture may include: (i) manual, mechanical, thermal, electrical, and electromagnetic treatments based on traditional Oriental medical diagnosis and concepts; and (ii) the recommendation of dietary guidelines and therapeutic exercise based on traditional Oriental medical diagnosis and concepts. "Practice of acupuncture" does not include: (i) the manual "manipulation or adjustment of the joints of the human body beyond the elastic barrier; or (ii) the manipulation of the articulation of the spinal column as defined in Section 58-73-102.*

The treatment of animals is not within the scope of practice.

Homeopathy is within the scope of practice of acupuncture.

Eligibility Requirements for Licensure

Formal Education Requirements: None.

Undergraduate Requirements: None

Apprenticeship a route of eligibility: Yes.

Experience: Yes.

NCCAOM Credentials Documentation Review Accepted: Yes.

Other Eligibility Requirements: Current and active NCCAOM certification.

Written Exam: The NCCAOM exam. A state jurisprudence examination is also required.

UTAH

Practical Exam: The NCCAOM PEPLS is required.

Reciprocity/Endorsement: The division may issue a license without examination to a person who has been in any state, district or territory of the United States or in any foreign country, whose education, experience and examination requirements are, or were at the time the license was issued, equal to those of Utah. Before any person may be issued a license under this section, he or she must produce satisfactory evidence of his or her qualifications, identity, and good standing in his or her occupation or profession.

Chemical Dependency Specialists

There is no provision for the practice of acupuncture by chemical dependency specialists.

Malpractice Insurance Requirement

Professional liability insurance is not mandated.

Health Insurance Coverage

Neither third party reimbursement nor reimbursement under workers' compensation is mandated.

Continuing Education Requirement

None at this time, but the division is planning to require current NCCAOM diplomate status for renewal, which means the licensee must meet the NCCAOM requirements for continuing education.

Supervision or Referral Requirement

None.

Practice of Acupuncture by Other Healthcare Providers

Medical doctors who practice acupuncture must represent themselves as medical doctors practicing acupuncture and not as acupuncturists.

Information Provided by the State Board of Medical Examiners in 2004: Medical doctors and osteopaths may practice acupuncture.

Information Provided by the State Board of Chiropractic Examiners in 2000: The scope of practice for chiropractors specifies that a chiropractor may practice acupuncture. A chiropractic physician may not claim to be a licensed acupuncturist without acupuncture licensure.

Notes

The practitioner must obtain signed inform consent from each patient.

VERMONT

Year first statute passed: 1985

Statute #: Title 26, Sections 3401-3412

Regulatory Agency Contact:
Ms. Loris Rollins, Unit Administrator
Office of Professional Regulation
26 Terrace Street, Drawer 09
Montpelier, VT 05609-1106
(802) 828-2191
(802) 828-2465 FAX
www.vtprofessionals.org

 # Licensed Practitioners: 111

Title of license:
Licensed Acupuncturist

Use of titles:
Certified acupuncture detoxification assistants may not use the title "acupuncturist" or "licensed acupuncturist.

Fees: Initial License $100
       Biennial Renewal $175

Governing Body

Office of Professional Regulation. Two licensed acupuncturists, appointed by the Secretary of State, serve as advisors to the director of the office on matters relating to acupuncture.

Definition of Acupuncture

According to statute—*"acupuncture" or the "practice of acupuncture" means the insertion of fine needles through the skin at certain points on the body, with or without the application of electric current or the application of heat to the needles or skin, or both, for the purpose of promoting health and balance as defined by traditional and modern Oriental theories. Acupuncture involves the use of traditional and modern Oriental diagnostic techniques, acupuncture therapy, and adjunctive therapies, including but not limited to: nonprescription remedies, exercise, nutritional and herbal therapies, therapeutic massage, and lifestyle counseling.*

The treatment of animals is not within the scope of practice. An acupuncturist may assist a licensed veterinarian in treating animals but only when the treatment has been prescribed by the veterinarian and the treatment is provided under the veterinarian's on-premises supervision.

Homeopathy is considered to be the practice of medicine.

Eligibility Requirements for Licensure

Two Routes of Eligibility

a) Formal Education: Completion of a three-year program in acupuncture and Oriental medicine with a minimum of 1,750 hours of entry-level acupuncture education, including 800 hours of clinical practice, 700 hours of Oriental medical theory, and 225 hours of biomedical sciences. The program must be ACAOM accredited or approved by the director of the office.

b) Training Program: A minimum of 40 points in any one of the following categories or combination of categories: a) apprenticeship–10 points for each 1,000 documented contact hours, up to a maximum of 13.5 points per year; b) completed academic work–5 points for each half-semester (minimum of 250 hours) completed with at least a 'C' or passing grade in the the field of acupuncture and Oriental medicine, up to a maximum of four periods or 20 points; 3) self-directed study–10 points for study equivalent to one year of full-time academic work in acupuncture and Oriental medicine, for a maximum of two years or 20 points.

VERMONT

Undergraduate Requirements: None.

NCCAOM Credentials Documentation Review Accepted: No.

Other Eligibility Requirements: Successful completion of the clean needle technique course offered by the Council of Colleges of Acupuncture and Oriental Medicine.

Written Exam: The NCCAOM examination in acupuncture.

Practical Exam: None specified.

Reciprocity/Endorsement: An applicant must be licensed or certified in good standing in another jurisdiction in which the standards and qualifications required for regulation in that district are at least equal to those required by Vermont.

Supervision or Referral Requirement

None.

Chemical Dependency Specialists

To be certified as an "acupuncture detoxification assistant," an applicant must have successfully completed the National Acupuncture Detoxification Association (NADA) training or training that meets or exceeds NADA standards. A certified acupuncture detoxification assistant may employ only the five-needle auricular protocol as described and located by NADA under the supervision of a licensed acupuncturist who is NADA certified in a state, federal, or other site approved by the director of the office.

Health Insurance Coverage

Neither third party reimbursement nor reimbursement under workers' compensation is mandated.

Practice of Acupuncture by Other Healthcare Providers

Information Provided by the Board of Medical Practice in 2004: Acupuncture is within the scope of practice of medical doctors and osteopaths.

Information Provided by the Board of Chiropractic Examination and Registration in 2004: Acupuncture is within the scope of practice of a chiropractor.

Continuing Education Requirement

Upon biennial renewal: 30 hours of continuing education. Research and writing, teaching, and distance learning are all eligible categories of continuing education upon approval from the director of the Office of Professional Regulation.

Malpractice Insurance Requirement

Professional liability insurance is not mandated.

Notes

Acupuncturists must disclose to each new client before the first treatment the acupuncturist's professional qualifications and experience, those actions that constitute unprofessional conduct, the method for filing a complaint or making a consumer inquiry and provisions relating to the manner in which the information shall be displayed and signed by both the acupuncturist and the client.

VIRGINIA

Year first statute passed: 1993

Statute #: 54.1-2900; 54.1-2956.9; 54.1-2956.10

Regulatory Agency Contact:
Ms. Ola Powers/Ms. Pam Nicholson
Virginia Board of Medicine
6603 West Broad Street, 5th Floor
Richmond, VA 23230-1712
(804) 662-7405
(804) 662-7281 FAX
www.dhp.virginia.gov

 # Licensed Practitioners: 256

Title of license:
Licensed Acupuncturist

Use of titles:
Regulations restrict licensed acupuncturists from using the titles "physician" or "doctor" in their practice.

Fees: Initial License $130
        Biennial Renewal $135

Governing Body

Board of Medicine. The Advisory Board on Acupuncture, under the Board of Medicine, is composed of five members: one doctor of medicine, osteopathy or podiatry who are licensed to practice acupuncture in Virginia, three licensed acupuncturists and one member of the public.

Definition of Acupuncture

According to statute—*practice of acupuncture means the stimulation of certain points on or near the surface of the body by the insertion of needles to prevent or modify the perception of pain or to normalize physiological functions, including pain control, for the treatment of certain ailments or conditions of the body and includes the techniques of electroacupuncture, cupping and moxibustion. The practice of acupuncture does not include the use of physical therapy, chiropractic, osteopathic manipulative techniques nor the use or prescribing of any drugs, medications, serums or vaccines.*

Whether the treatment of animals is within the scope of practice has not been determined.

Whether homeopathy is within the scope of practice of acupuncture has not been determined. It is the practice of medicine.

Eligibility Requirements for Licensure

Formal Education Requirements: Graduation from a ACAOM-accredited program of at least 1,000 hours including 700 didactic and 250 clinical hours in no less than eighteen months. Individuals who graduated after July 1, 1990 must document 90 semester credit hours of full-time study.

An applicant who graduated from an acupuncture program that is in candidacy with ACAOM shall be eligible for licensure provided the program is subsequently granted accreditation within three years of the applicant's graduation.

An applicant who graduated from a school not accredited by ACAOM must have completed a course of study equivalent to graduates of approved institutions.

Apprenticeship: Not a route of eligibility.

VIRGINIA

Experience: Not a route of eligibility.

NCCAOM Credentials Documentation Review Accepted: The NCCAOM CDR is accepted in lieu of the acupuncture theory portion of the examination. Applicants must still pass the PEPLS and the CCAOM clean needle technique course.

Other Eligibility Requirements: An individual must also complete a CCAOM clean needle technique course. Applicants who are foreign educated must demonstrate a satisfactory score on either the TOEFL or the TSE. An applicant applying to practice as an acupuncturist whose native language is not English and whose acupuncture education was also not in English shall be exempt from the requirement for TSE or TOEFL if the majority of his clients speak the language of the acupuncturist.

Written Exam: The NCCAOM exam in acupuncture.

Practical Exam: the NCCAOM PEPLS.

Reciprocity/Endorsement: No.

Supervision or Referral Requirement

The regulations specify that a request for acupuncture services shall be accompanied by a diagnosis of the ailment or condition to be treated by the licensed acupuncturist from a licensed physician based on his or her examination of the patient within the past six months. The acupuncturist must report back to the referring physician after three months or ten treatments, whichever occurs first.

Chemical Dependency Specialists

According to statute—*"Auricular acupuncture" means the subcutaneous insertion of sterile, disposable acupuncture needles in predetermined, bilateral locations in the outer ear when used exclusively and specifically in the context of an approved chemical dependency treatment program, under the appropriate supervision of a licensed physician acupuncturist or licensed acupuncturist.*

Malpractice Insurance Requirement

Professional liability insurance is not mandated.

Continuing Education Requirement

Upon biennial renewal: active status NCCAOM certification in acupuncture.

Practice of Acupuncture by Other Healthcare Providers

Information Provided by the Virginia Board of Medicine in 2004: In order to qualify to practice acupuncture, licensed doctors of medicine, osteopathy, podiatry, and chiropractic shall have first obtained at least 200 hours of instruction in basic aspects of the practice of acupuncture, specific uses and teaching of acupuncture, and indications and contraindications for acupuncture administration. A podiatrist may use acupuncture only for treatment of pain syndromes originating in the human foot.

Health Insurance Coverage

If a third party payer reimburses a medical doctor for acupuncture treatment it must also reimburse a licensed acupuncturist.

Notes

Regulations require that disposable needles be used and discarded after each patient treatment.

WASHINGTON

Year first statute passed: 1985

Statute #: 18.06

Regulatory Agency Contact:
Ms. Vicki Brown
Department of Health
Health Professions Quality Assurance
310 Israel Road
PO Box 47860
Tumwater WA 98501-7860
(360) 236-4865
(360) 664-9077 FAX
www.dol.wa.gov/main/biglist.htm

 # Licensed Practitioners: 904

Title of license:
Licensed Acupuncturist

Use of titles:
An acupuncturist may not use the titles "Dr.," "Doctor," or "Ph.D." unless the nature of the degree is clearly stated.

Fees: Application &
Initial License $50
Annual Renewal $90

Governing Body

Department of Health.

Definition of Acupuncture

According to statute—*acupuncture means a healthcare service based on an Oriental system of medical theory utilizing Oriental diagnosis and treatment to promote health and treat organic or functional disorders by treating specific acupuncture points or meridians.*

Acupuncture includes the following techniques: acupuncture needles, electrical, mechanical, or magnetic devices, moxibustion, acupressure, cupping, dermal friction, infra-red, sonopuncture, laserpuncture, dietary advice based on Oriental medical theory, point injection therapy (aquapuncture).

The treatment of animals is not within the scope of practice.

Whether homeopathy is within the scope of practice of acupuncture has not been determined.

Eligibility Requirements for Licensure

Formal Education Requirements: Two years of academic coursework including anatomy, physiology, microbiology, biochemistry, pathology, hygiene and a survey of western clinical sciences and successful completion of 500 hours of clinical training in acupuncture that is approved by the department. The rules specify 45 academic credits of western science (450 hours) plus CPR and 75 credits of acupuncture sciences (750 hours). The school must be approved by the department or be accredited by ACAOM.

Undergraduate Requirements: None.

Apprenticeship: Similar to formal education requirements.

Experience: Not a route of eligibility.

NCCAOM Credentials Documentation Review Accepted: No.

Other Eligibility Requirements: Each applicant must demonstrate sufficient fluency in reading, speaking, and understanding the English language to enable the applicant to communicate with other healthcare providers and patients concerning healthcare problems and treatment. The NCCAOM exam and clean needle technique course in English fulfill this requirement, as does a TOEFL score of 550.

Written Exam: The NCCAOM written exam.

Practical Exam: The NCCAOM PFPLS exam.

Reciprocity/Endorsement: Endorsement is possible if the licensure requirements of the other state are equivalent to, or greater than, those of Washington state.

Supervision or Referral Requirement

Consultation or referral for specific conditions.

When an acupuncturist sees a patient with potentially serious disorders such as cardiac conditions, acute abdominal symptoms, and such other conditions, the acupuncturist shall immediately request a consultation or recent written diagnosis from a physician licensed under chapter 18.71 or 18.57 RCW. In the event that the patient with the disorder refuses to authorize such consultation or provide a recent diagnosis from such physician, acupuncture treatment shall not be continued.

The rules add to the list of conditions: uncontrolled hypertension, acute undiagnosed neurological changes, suspected fracture or dislocation, acute respiratory distress without prior history, unexplained weight loss or gain in excess of fifteen percent of body weight within a three-month period, and suspected systemic infection.

A consultation plan, which lists medical or osteopathic doctors available for referral, must be filed with the state.

Practice of Acupuncture by Other Healthcare Providers

Exemption language is provided in two instances: a) if the individual is credentialed under the laws of Washington and is performing services within his or her authorized scope of practice or b) practice by an individual employed by the U.S. government while engaged in the performance of duties prescribed by the laws of the United States.

Information Provided by the Department of Health in 2004: Acupuncture is within the scope of practice of medical doctors and osteopaths. No specific training requirements have been set.

Acupuncture is not within the scope of practice of podiatrists.

Information Provided by the Board of Chiropractic in 2000: Acupuncture is not within the scope of practice of chiropractic. In order for a chiropractor to practice acupuncture, he or she must meet the requirements in the acupuncture law. If a chiropractor is also licensed as an acupuncturist, he or she must at all times differentiate chiropractic care from acupuncture care.

Health Insurance Coverage

All third party payers in the state, with the exception of the state Basic Health Plan and self-capitated plans, must reimburse acupuncturists.

Chemical Dependency Specialists

There is no provision for the practice of acupuncture by chemical dependency specialists.

Malpractice Insurance Requirement

Professional liability insurance is not mandated.

Continuing Education Requirement

None.

Notes

*Legislation in 2003—new rules are being written regarding the nature of the required clinical training.

WEST VIRGINIA

Year first statute passed: 1996	**# Licensed Practitioners:** 44

Statute #: 54

Regulatory Agency Contact:
Mr. C.P. Negri, President
Board of Acupuncture
364 High Street, Suite 203
Morgantown, WV 26505
(304) 529-4558
(304) 529-3710 FAX
www.wvs.state.wv.us/acupuncture

Title of license:
Acupuncturist

Use of titles:
Per the Board of Acupuncture: the titles "licensed acupuncturist," "acupuncture physician," or "Oriental medical doctor" are permitted.

Fees:
	Application	$75
	Initial License	$425
	Biennial Renewal	$425

Governing Body

The Board of Acupuncture consists of five members appointed by the governor with the advice and consent of the Senate. Three shall be licensed acupuncturist, one is a public member and one is a licensed physician.

Definition of Acupuncture

According to statute—*"acupuncture" means a form of healthcare, based on a theory of energetic physiology, that describes the interrelationship of the body organs or functions with an associated point or combination of points. "Practice Acupuncture" means the use of Oriental medical therapies for the purpose of normalizing energetic physiological functions including pain control, and for the promotion, maintenance and restoration of health.*

Scope of practice includes the stimulation of points of the body by the insertion of acupuncture needles, the application of moxibustion and manual, mechanical, thermal or electrical therapies only when performed in accordance with the principles of oriental acupuncture medical theories. The ethical provisions in the rules regarding the sale of Oriental medicines in the office provide that Oriental medicine which may be prescribed by licensed acupuncturists include, but are not limited to: herbs, alone and in combinations, glandulars, minerals, vitamins and Chinese patent medicines. (Section 32-10-4)

The treatment of animals is not within the scope of practice.

Homeopathy is within the scope of practice.

Eligibility Requirements for Licensure

Formal Education Requirements: Graduation from a course of training of at least 1,800 hours, including 300 clinical hours, that is either approved by ACAOM or found by the board to be equivalent to a course approved by ACAOM.

Undergraduate Requirements: None.

Apprenticeship: Completion of an apprenticeship consisting of at least 2,700 hours within a five-year period under an individual approved by that jurisdiction to perform acupuncture.

Experience: Practice of acupuncture in accordance with the law of another jurisdiction or jurisdictions for a period of at least three years within the five years immediately prior to application that consisted of at least 500 patient visits per year.

NCCAOM Credentials Documentation Review Accepted: No.

Other Eligibility Requirements: An applicant must be of good moral character and at least 18 years of age.

Written Exam: The NCCAOM examination or on an examination determined by the board to be equivalent to the NCCAOM examination is one route of eligibility.

Practical Exam: None specified.

Reciprocity/Endorsement: The acupuncture board may grant licenses by reciprocity but this may only be done for states which permit reciprocity for acupuncturists in West Virginia.

Supervision or Referral Requirement

None.

Malpractice Insurance Requirement

Professional liability insurance or surety bond of at least $10,000/ 30,000.

Health Insurance Coverage

Both third party reimbursement and reimbursement under workers' compensation is mandated.

Continuing Education Requirement

Upon biennial renewal: 48 hours of continuing education. Hours in practice management are limited to 12 hours per period. Distance learning is accepted.

Chemical Dependency Specialists

There is no provision for the practice of acupuncture by chemical dependency specialists.

Practice of Acupuncture by Other Healthcare Providers

The provisions of the acupuncture statute do not limit, preclude or otherwise interfere with the practice of other healthcare providers working in any setting and licensed by appropriate agencies or boards of the state of West Virginia whose practices and training may include elements of the same nature as the practice of a licensed acupuncturist.

Information Provided by the West Virginia Board of Medicine in 2004: The board of medicine has not set any specific training requirements for an M.D. to practice acupuncture

A physician assistant may not practice acupuncture. (11 CSR 1B 2.6.13)

Information Provided by the State Board of Chiropractic Examiners in 2004: Acupuncture is within the scope of practice of chiropractors. In order to practice acupuncture, a chiropractor must have 100 hours of training taught through an accredited chiropractic college.

Notes

Patient informed consent is required.

An acupuncturist who wishes to dispense herbs, vitamins, minerals, homeopathic drugs, glandulars and extracts of glands, formulas and compounds, and legend drugs to patients must register with the board as a "dispensing acupuncturist."

WISCONSIN

Year first statute passed: 1989

Statute #: 451

Regulatory Agency Contact:
Dr. Kimberly M. Nania, Director
Cathy Pond, Credentialing Administrator
Department of Regulation and Licensing
Bureau of Health Service Professions
Acupuncture Certification
1400 East Washington Avenue
Madison, WI 53708-8935
(608) 266-2112
(608) 267-3816 FAX
http://drl.wi.gov

 # Licensed Practitioners: 312

Title of license:
Acupuncturist

Use of titles:
Licensees may use any initials for which they have credentials.

Fees: Initial License $53
          Biennial Renewal $70

Governing Body

Department of Regulation and Licensing. The Department utilizes an advisory committee of acupuncturists to assist in the regulation of the field.

Definition of Acupuncture

According to statute—*acupuncture means promoting, maintaining or restoring health or diagnosing, preventing or treating disease based on traditional Oriental medical concepts of treating specific areas of the human body, known as acupuncture points or meridians, by performing any of the following practices: (a) Inserting acupuncture needles. (b) Moxibustion. (c) Applying manual, thermal or electrical stimulation or any other secondary therapeutic technique.*

Homeopathy is not within the scope of practice.

The treatment of animals is not within the scope of practice

Eligibility Requirements for Licensure

Formal Education Requirements: Completion of a course of study and residency the equivalent of at least two consecutive years of full time education and clinical work in Oriental diagnostic and therapeutic theories and practices at a school accredited by the ACAOM or the NCCAOM.

Undergraduate Requirements: None.

Apprenticeship: Not a route of eligibility.

Experience: Not a route of eligibility.

NCCAOM Credentials Documentation Review Accepted: No. The NCCAOM exam is required.

Other Eligibility Requirements: Successful completion of a clean needle technique course acceptable to the department.

WISCONSIN

Written Exam: The NCCAOM examination and an acceptable clean needle technique course and exam is required.

Practical Exam: None specified.

Reciprocity/Endorsement: Applicants must be licensees from states with substantially equivalent requirements and have a minimum of five years of practice in the United States immediately prior to application with a minimum of 500 patient visits on 100 patients within the last twelve months, 70% of which must be in general healthcare.

Supervision or Referral Requirement

None.

Continuing Education Requirement

None.

Practice of Acupuncture by Other Healthcare Providers

Information Provided by the Board of Medical Examiners in 2000: Acupuncture is within the scope of practice of medical doctors, osteopaths, podiatrists, and physician assistants. No specific training is necessary.

Information Provided by the Board of Chiropractic Examiners in 2004: Chiropractors may not practice acupuncture under their scope of practice.

Malpractice Insurance Requirement

Professional liability insurance is not mandated.

Health Insurance Coverage

Neither third party reimbursement nor reimbursement under workers' compensation is mandated.

Chemical Dependency Specialists

There is no provision for the practice of acupuncture by chemical dependency specialists.

Notes

Patient informed consent for treatment is required.

WYOMING

Year first statute passed: N/A	**# Licensed Practitioners:** N/A
Statute #: N/A	**Title of license:** N/A
Governing Body: N/A	

There is no practice act for acupuncturists

Information Provided by the Board of Medicine in 2004

Acupuncture is not regulated in Wyoming.

Information Provided by the Board of Chiropractic Examiners in 2000

The State Board of Chiropractic Examiners wrote a letter to its licensees, dated January 20, 1997, concluding–"It is our view that chiropractors should not be permitted to practice acupuncture absent express statutory authority to do so."

TABLES
&
RESOURCES

Table 1.
Chronology of First Acupuncture Practice Laws and
Reported Number of Licensees in Each State

The states are listed in chronological order according to the year the first acupuncture practice act was passed in that state. The columns of dates across the top represent the years in which data was gathered for this and previous editions of this publication.

The numbers in each column represent reported numbers of licensees for that year for the corresponding state.

It should be noted that some individuals are licensed in more than one state and that the figures reported in this chart represent the numbers of active licenses reported in each state.

The information contained in this, and other tables, is subject to change at any time. The reader is advised to contact individual state boards for the most current and complete information.

TABLE 1. CHRONOLOGY OF FIRST ACUPUNCTURE PRACTICE LAWS AND REPORTED NUMBER OF LICENSEES IN EACH STATE

1st Law Passed	State	1992	1993	1994	1996	1998	2000	2004
1973	Maryland	313	259	259	433	433	720	740
	Nevada	30	30	30	30	30	29	43
	Oregon	143	168	168	256	334	326	576
1974	Hawaii	252	270	276	338	356	405	532
	Montana	68	68	68	92	98	117	136
	South Carolina	1	1	1	2	73	73	47
1975	Louisiana		1	2	2	3	3	12
	California	2,798	2,829	3,049	3,692	4,387	5,321	8,566
1978	Rhode Island	24	24	45	60	79	99	131
1981	Florida	399	399	442	537	810	1,029	1,580
	New Mexico	270	270	270	390	390	498	533
1983	New Jersey	45	45	45	62	101	180	367
	Utah	22	22	22	27	27	37	64
1985	Vermont				34	52	76	111
	Washington	137	144	169	299	274	535	904
1986	Massachusetts	356	398	434	524	652	805	941
	Pennsylvania	105	105	249	310	310	545	583
1987	Maine	38	39	45	53	59	79	90
1989	Colorado	93	115	143	202	293	386	711
	District of Columbia	42	42	42	42	117	128	176
	Wisconsin	80	99	108	172	165	133	312
1990	Alaska	9	12	14	28	38	47	62
1991	New York	300	300	500	700	800	1,200	2,400
1993	Iowa				3	8	19	27
	North Carolina			7	67	115	146	227
	Texas			154	300	363	409	627
	Virginia			3	14	31	80	256
1995	Connecticut				8	98	163	257
	Minnesota				13	88	119	316
1996	West Virginia				4	30	40	44
1997	Arkansas					9	17	26
	Illinois						224	421
	New Hampshire						34	78
1998	Arizona						142	314
	Missouri							57
1999	Idaho						45	75
	Indiana							48
2000	Georgia						8	132
	Ohio						11	69
	Tennessee							69
2001	Nebraska							11
	Totals	**5,525**	**5,640**	**6,545**	**8,694**	**10,623**	**14,228**	**22,671**

2005 National Acupuncture Foundation / www.nationalacupuncturefoundation.org

Table 2.
Regulatory Agencies Governing Acupuncture Practice

This table lists the states that have acupuncture practice acts and indicates the corresponding type of regulatory agency that administers the professional regulation of acupuncture.

The information contained in this, and other tables, is subject to change at any time. The reader is advised to contact individual state boards for the most current and complete information.

TABLE 2. REGULATORY AGENCIES GOVERNING ACUPUNCTURE PRACTICE

State	Independent Board for Acupuncture	Regulated Under Other Agency	Advisory Committee for Acupuncture
Alaska		✔	
Arizona	✔		
Arkansas	✔		
California	✔		
Colorado		✔	
Connecticut		✔	
District of Columbia		✔	✔
Florida	✔		
Georgia		✔	✔
Hawaii	✔		
Idaho	✔		
Illinois		✔	✔
Indiana		✔	✔
Iowa		✔	
Louisiana		✔	
Maine		Joint Board	
Maryland	✔		
Massachusetts		✔	✔
Minnesota		✔	✔
Missouri		✔	✔
Montana		✔	
Nebraska		✔	
Nevada	✔		
New Hampshire	✔		
New Jersey		✔	✔
New Mexico	✔		
New York		✔	✔
North Carolina	✔		
Ohio		✔	
Oregon		✔	✔
Pennsylvania		✔	
Rhode Island		✔	
South Carolina		✔	
Tennessee		✔	✔
Texas		✔	✔
Utah		✔	✔
Vermont		✔	✔
Virginia		✔	✔
Washington		✔	
West Virginia	✔		
Wisconsin		✔	✔

2005 National Acupuncture Foundation / www.nationalacupuncturefoundation.org

Table 3.
Scope of Practice Inclusions Specified in Statute or Rule

This table provides a comparison of the most common inclusions in the scope of practice of acupuncture specifically mentioned in statute or rule. Additional notes are made of other specifically mentioned procedures or practices in the "Other" column. However, no attempt has been made to interpret terms, such as "adjunctive therapies" if they are not specifically defined in statute or rule. Also, some definitions of scope are too extensive to list all techniques, tools, methods or practices included.

A plus sign (+) indicates that additional information on scope may be found in the specific state listing.

An asterisk (*) in a cell is a direction to special information in the "Other" column for reference.

This is not meant to be an exhaustive representation of scope of practice for acupuncturists in every state listed. As mentioned in the chapter on regulation in this book, terms such as "Oriental medical therapies" or "adjunctive therapies" may allow for interpretation by the regulating agency.

The information contained in this, and other tables, is subject to change at any time. The reader is advised to contact individual state boards for the most current and complete information.

TABLE 3. SCOPE OF PRACTICE INCLUSIONS SPECIFIED IN LICENSING STATUTE OR RULE

State	Acupuncture Only	Herbs	Recommendation Diet or Supplements	Other
Alaska			✔	
Arizona		topical	✔	therapeutic exercise
Arkansas		✔	✔	homeopathy, western diagnostics, injection therapy, +
California		✔	✔	Oriental massage, magnets
Colorado		✔	✔	specifically excluded: western diagnostic tests
Connecticut	✔			
District of Columbia	✔			
Florida		✔	✔	homeopathy, Oriental massage, Qi gong, +
Georgia		✔	✔	
Hawaii		✔		
Idaho		✔	✔	therapeutic exercise, +
Illinois	✔			
Indiana				"adjunctive therapies and diagnostic techniques"
Iowa				"adjunctive therapies and diagnostic techniques"
Louisiana	✔ *			*acupuncture is the practice of medicine
Maine		✔ *	✔	*certification in herbology required
Maryland				"Oriental medical therapies"
Massachusetts		✔ *		*certification in herbology required; extensive inclusions
Minnesota		✔	✔	Oriental massage, exercise, breathing techniques
Missouri	✔			
Montana		✔	✔	
Nebraska		✔		
Nevada		✔ *		*certification in herbology required, +
New Hampshire		✔	✔	homeopathy, massage, life-style counseling, +
New Jersey		✔		gwa-sha, magnets, cupping+
New Mexico		✔	✔	homeopathy; Extended & Expanded prescriptive authority
New York	✔			
North Carolina		✔	✔	massage, therapeutic exercise, +
Ohio	✔			
Oregon		✔	✔	Oriental massage, exercise, +
Pennsylvania		✔	✔	massage
Rhode Island	✔			
South Carolina				no defined scope
Tennessee			✔	therapeutic exercise
Texas		✔ *	✔	*certification in herbology required
Utah			✔	therapeutic exercise
Vermont		✔	✔	massage, +
Virginia	✔			
Washington			✔	point injection therapy+
West Virginia		✔ *	✔	*"dispensing" acupuncturists must register
Wisconsin	✔			

Please see individual state listings for details, limitations, and specific language.
2005 National Acupuncture Foundation / www.nationalacupuncturefoundation.org

Table 4.
Educational Requirements for Licensure

This table summarizes current educational requirements for licensure in each state.

A checkmark (✔) in the column **ACAOM Standard**, means that the educational requirements meet the current standards for accredited programs through the Accreditation Commission for Acupuncture and Oriental Medicine.

A checkmark (✔) in the column **Exceeds ACAOM**, means that the educational requirements for licensure in that state exceed ACAOM's standards for the scope of practice allowed in that state. For instance, the scope of practice in Rhode Island includes only the practice of acupuncture and the educational requirement for licensure in Rhode Island (2,500 hours) exceeds ACAOM's standard for acupuncture programs (1,905 hours). In the case of New Mexico, the overall number of hours is within ACAOM standards for acupuncture and Oriental medicine programs, but New Mexico's requirement of 900 clinical hours is in excess of ACAOM's standard for clinical hours.

The notes should be read in the following manner:

"Bacc." = Baccalaureate degree

"ACAOM specified"— either statute or rule has specifically designated ACAOM standards. Most states also designate program length and/or number of hours of education required. This has also been noted.

"Accredited program specified"— note that the check mark accompanying this notation is in the **ACAOM Standard** column. Although ACAOM is not specified in these states, it is currently the only agency recognized by the U.S. Department of Education for accrediting acupuncture and Oriental medine programs, therefore ACAOM standards are specified by default.

"board-approved" program — the state makes no reference in statute or rule to ACAOM or accreditation of educational programs. They may or may not meet ACAOM standards.

"by virtue of NCCAOM requirements"—although ACAOM or accreditation is not specifically mentioned, exam and/or certification through the NCCAOM is, and NCCAOM requires graduation from an ACAOM-accredited program to sit the certification exam.

Although a majority of states have adopted ACAOM standards, many of those states further define program length and/or hours of education required ranging from 2-year to 4-year programs and/or 1,000 to 2,500 hours. While most of these state requirements are consistent with the level of education for current students and recent graduates, some exceed the educational standards of ten to twenty years ago. Some states have made provision for practitioners who graduated prior to the current standards in their rules, but most have not.

The information contained in this, and other tables, is subject to change at any time. The reader is advised to contact individual state boards for the most current and complete information.

TABLE 4. EDUCATIONAL REQUIREMENTS
FOR LICENSURE

States	Current Educational Requirements			Notes
	Undergrad Reqs	**ACAOM Standard**	**Exceeds ACAOM**	
Alaska		✔		ACAOM specified
Arizona				board-approved 1,850 hours
Arkansas		✔		ACAOM specified / 4-yr program
California	60 hrs		✔	3,000 hrs
Colorado		✔		by virtue of NCCAOM requirements
Connecticut	60 hrs	✔		Accredited program specified / 1,350 hrs
District of Columbia		✔		ACAOM specified / 3-yr program
Florida	60 hrs		✔	2,700 hrs/Allows for evolution of standards
Georgia		✔		by virtue of NCCAOM requirements
Hawaii		✔		Accredited program specified / 2,175 hrs
Idaho		✔		by virtue of NCCAOM requirements
Illinois		✔		by virtue of NCCAOM requirements
Indiana		✔		ACAOM specified / 3-yr program
Iowa		✔		ACAOM specified / 3-yr program
Louisiana				board-approved 36 months training
Maine	Bacc.			board approved 1,000 hrs
Maryland		✔		ACAOM specified / 1,800 hrs
Massachusetts	2 yrs	✔		ACAOM specified / 1,350 hrs
Minnesota		✔		by virtue of NCCAOM requirements
Missouri		✔		by virtue of NCCAOM requirements
Montana		✔		ACAOM specified / 1,000 hrs
Nebraska		✔		ACAOM specified / 1,725 hrs
Nevada	Bacc.		✔	3,000 hrs
New Hampshire	Bacc.	✔		ACAOM specified
New Jersey	Bacc.			board-approved two-year program
New Mexico			✔	900 hrs clinic
New York	60 hrs	✔		ACAOM specified / 3-yr program
North Carolina		✔		ACAOM specified / 3-yr program
Ohio		✔		by virtue of NCCAOM requirements
Oregon		✔		ACAOM specified
Pennsylvania	2 yrs	✔		Accredited program specified
Rhode Island			✔	ACAOM specified / 2,500 hrs
South Carolina		✔		by virtue of NCCAOM requirements
Tennessee		✔		ACAOM specified / 3-yr program
Texas	60 hrs	✔		ACAOM specified / 1,800 hrs.
Utah		✔		by virtue of NCCAOM requirements
Vermont		✔		ACAOM specified / 1,750 hrs
Virginia		✔		ACAOM specified / 1,000 hrs
Washington		✔		ACAOM specified / 2-yr program
West Virginia		✔		ACAOM specified / 1,800 hrs
Wisconsin		✔		ACAOM specified / 2-yr program

Please see individual state listings for details, limitations, and specific language
2005 National Acupuncture Foundation / www.nationalacupuncturefoundation.org

Table 5.
Continuing Education Requirements for Licensure Renewal

All states but one—New York—are either on an annual or biennial renewal schedule. New York is on a triennial schedule. In some states, it the renewal schedule, whether annual or biennial, is based on the calendar year, in some on the anniversary date of first licensure, and in others on the licensee's birth date. Contact the appropriate state agency for information on their renewal schedule.

In those states that require current, active NCCAOM certification status, the continuing education requirement is based on the NCCAOM's requirements for active certification.

The information contained in this, and other tables, is subject to change at any time. The reader is advised to contact individual state boards for the most current and complete information.

TABLE 5. CONTINUING EDUCATION REQUIREMENTS FOR ACUPUNCTURE LICENSURE

State	CEU hours on Annual Renewal	CEU hours on Biennial Renewal	Current Active NCCAOM	Other
Alaska		15		
Arizona		15		
Arkansas		24		
California		30		
Colorado	0			
Connecticut		0		
District of Columbia		0		
Florida		30		
Georgia		0		
Hawaii		0		
Idaho	15			
Illinois		30		
Indiana			✔	
Iowa		30		
Louisiana	0			
Maine		30		
Maryland		40		
Massachusetts		30		
Minnesota			✔	
Missouri		*	✔	
Montana	0			
Nebraska		50	✔	
Nevada	10			
New Hampshire		30		
New Jersey		20		
New Mexico	15*			*add reqs for EP authority
New York				*Triennial renewal; no CE req.
North Carolina		40		
Ohio			✔	
Oregon	0			
Pennsylvania		0		
Rhode Island	20			
South Carolina			✔	
Tennessee		0		
Texas	17			
Utah		0*		*see state listing
Vermont		30		
Virginia			✔	
Washington	0			
West Virginia		48		
Wisconsin		0		

Please see individual state listings for details, limitations, and specific language
2005 National Acupuncture Foundation / www.nationalacupuncturefoundation.org

Table 6.
Supervision and/or Referral Requirements

A check mark (✔) indicates that this category of supervision, referral, or prior diagnosis is required in the corresponding state.

A cell with no check mark in it indicates that a state agency has confirmed that this category of supervision, referral, or prior diagnosis is not required in the corresponding state.

The information contained in this, and other tables, is subject to change at any time. The reader is advised to contact individual state boards for the most current and complete information.

TABLE 6. SUPERVISION AND/OR REFERRAL REQUIREMENTS

State	Referral	Supervision	Prior Diagnosis	Notes
Alaska				
Arizona				
Arkansas				
California				
Colorado				
Connecticut				
District of Columbia				Requirement removed in 2004
Florida				
Georgia		✔ *		*first year practitioners only
Hawaii	✔ *			*for organic disorders only
Idaho				
Illinois				Requirement removed in 2004
Indiana	✔		✔	referral or diagnosis
Iowa				
Louisiana		✔		
Maine				
Maryland				
Massachusetts				
Minnesota				
Missouri				
Montana				
Nebraska	✔		✔	referral or diagnosis
Nevada				
New Hampshire				
New Jersey	✔		✔	referral or diagnosis
New Mexico				
New York				
North Carolina				
Ohio	✔	✔		
Oregon				
Pennsylvania	✔		✔	referral and diagnosis
Rhode Island				
South Carolina	✔	✔		
Tennessee				
Texas	✔		✔	
Utah				
Vermont				
Virginia	✔		✔	
Washington	✔ *			*for specific conditions only
West Virginia				
Wisconsin				

Please see individual state listings for details, limitations, and specific language
2005 National Acupuncture Foundation / www.nationalacupuncturefoundation.org

Table 7.
Insurance Reimbursement for Acupuncture and Malpractice Requirements for Acupuncturists

A check mark (✔) indicates that a state agency has confirmed the information.

A cell with no check mark in it indicates that this category of insurance is not mandated by the state at this time.

The information contained in this, and other tables, is subject to change at any time. The reader is advised to contact individual state boards for the most current and complete information.

TABLE 7. INSURANCE REIMBURSEMENT FOR ACUPUNCTURE AND MALPRACTICE INSURANCE REQUIREMENTS FOR ACUPUNCTURISTS

State	Reimbursement or Parity Mandated	Workers' Comp Mandated	Malpractice Insurance Required
Alaska			
Arizona			
Arkansas			
California	✔	✔	
Colorado			✔
Connecticut			
District of Columbia			
Florida	✔		✔
Georgia			✔
Hawaii			
Idaho			
Illinois			
Indiana			
Iowa			
Louisiana			
Maine	✔		
Maryland			
Massachusetts			
Minnesota			
Missouri			
Montana	✔	✔	
Nebraska			
Nevada	✔	✔	
New Hampshire			
New Jersey			
New Mexico			
New York			
North Carolina			
Ohio			
Oregon	✔	✔	
Pennsylvania			
Rhode Island			
South Carolina			
Tennessee			
Texas			
Utah			
Vermont			
Virginia	✔		
Washington	✔		
West Virginia	✔	✔	✔
Wisconsin			

2005 National Acupuncture Foundation / www.nationalacupuncturefoundation.org

Tables 8 & 9.
Acupuncture Specified in the Scope of Other Healthcare Practitioners

Tables 8 and 9 contain information regarding the practice of acupuncture within the scope of other healthcare practitioners. Please note the following when viewing this table.

A check mark (✔) indicates that a state regulatory agency has confirmed that the practice of acupuncture is within the scope of practice of this category of practitioner.

"**0**" indicates confirmation from a state regulatory agency that no specific training is required to practice acupuncture by this category of practitioner.

"**No**" indicates confirmation from a state regulatory agency that the practice of acupuncture is not within the scope of practice of this category of practitioner. This may have been determined by either specific reference as in–"acupuncture is not within the scope of practice of X category of practitioner," or through non-inclusion as in—"acupuncture may only be practiced by X category of practitioner."

A cell with no information in it indicates that the information was unavailable or undetermined at the time of research for this book. For instance, it may not yet be determined whether acupuncture is within the scope of practice of a particular category of practitioner; or, it may have been determined that acupuncture is within the scope of a certain category of practitioner, but not if, or what level of, training is required to practice; or, the information was not available at the time.

The information contained in this, and other tables, is subject to change at any time. The reader is advised to contact individual state boards for the most current and complete information.

TABLE 8. ACUPUNCTURE WITHIN THE SCOPE OF M.D./D.O./D.C.

State	M.D. D.O.	Training Specified	D.C.	Training Specified	Notes
Alabama	✔	0	✔	100 hrs*	*board-approved exam required
Alaska	✔	0	No		
Arizona	✔	0	✔	100 hrs*	*NBCE exam required
Arkansas	✔	0	No		
California	✔	0	No		
Colorado	✔	0	✔	100 hrs*	*includes supervised clinical
Connecticut	✔	0	✔	0	
Delaware	✔	0	✔	100 hrs	
District of Columbia	✔	250 hrs	✔	250 hrs	
Florida	✔	0	✔	100 hrs*	*NBCE exam required
Georgia	✔	300 hrs	No		
Hawaii	No		No		
Idaho	✔	0	✔	*	*must be certified by board of acupuncture
Illinois	✔	0	✔	0	
Indiana	✔	0	✔	200 hrs	title: "licensed professional acupuncturist"
Iowa	✔	0	✔	100 hrs*	*board-approved exam required
Kansas	✔	*	✔	*	*must be competent"
Kentucky	✔	0	No		
Louisiana	✔	6 mos	No		
Maine	✔	0	✔	200 hrs*	*board-approved exam required
Maryland	✔	250 hrs	No		
Massachusetts	✔	0	No		
Michigan	✔	0	No		
Minnesota	✔	0	✔	100 hrs*	*NBCE exam required
Missouri	✔	0	✔	100 hrs	
Mississippi	✔	"adequate"	No		
Montana	✔	0	✔		
Nebraska	✔	0	✔	0	
Nevada	✔	"adequate"	No		
New Hampshire	✔	0	✔		* see state listing; may not call it "acupuncture"
New Jersey	✔	300 hrs	No		
New Mexico	✔	"appropriate"	✔	0*	*new rules pending for 2005
New York	✔	300 hrs	No		
North Carolina	✔	"sufficient"	✔		
North Dakota	✔	0	✔	100 hrs	
Ohio	✔	0	No		
Oklahoma	✔	0	✔	0*	*voluntary registration
Oregon	✔	0	No		
Pennsylvania	✔	200 hrs	No		
Rhode Island	✔	300 hrs	No		
South Carolina	✔	0	No		
South Dakota	✔	0	✔	100 hrs*	*board-approved exam required
Tennessee	✔	0	No		
Texas	✔	0	✔	"properly"	
Utah	✔		✔		
Vermont	✔		✔		
Virginia	✔	200 hrs	✔	200 hrs	
Washington	✔	0	No		
West Virginia	✔	0	✔	100 hrs	
Wisconsin	✔	0	No		
Wyoming	✔	0	No		

TABLE 9. ACUPUNCTURE WITHIN THE SCOPE OF OTHER PROVIDERS

State	D.P.M.	Training Specified	D.D.S.	Training Specified	P.A.	Training Specified	N.D.	Training Specified	A.D.S.	Training Specified
Alabama	No		No		No		No			
Alaska	✓		✓	0						
Arizona					✓		✓	0	✓	meets or exceeds NADA
Arkansas									✓	
California	✓		✓	80 hrs						
Colorado					No					
Connecticut	✓	0	✓	0	✓		✓		✓	
Delaware	No		No		No		No			
District of Columbia										
Florida										
Georgia									✓	meets or exceeds NADA
Hawaii	No		No		No					
Idaho										
Illinois			✓	0	No					
Indiana	✓	200 hrs	✓	200 hrs					✓	meets or exceeds NADA
Iowa	✓	0	✓	0	No					
Kansas					✓		✓			
Kentucky										
Louisiana	No				No					
Maine					✓		✓	1,300 hrs		
Maryland			✓						✓	meets or exceeds NADA
Massachusetts	No				No					
Michigan	No		No		No					
Minnesota										
Missouri							✓		✓	
Mississippi										
Montana	✓		✓							
Nebraska	No				No					
Nevada										
New Hampshire							✓			
New Jersey	No		✓		No					
New Mexico					✓				✓	rules pending
New York	No		✓	300 hrs	No				✓	
North Carolina										
North Dakota	✓		✓							
Ohio										
Oklahoma										
Oregon	No				No					
Pennsylvania	✓		✓							
Rhode Island										
South Carolina	No		✓		No				✓	NADA certification
South Dakota										
Tennessee									✓	meets or exceeds NADA
Texas									✓	70 hrs
Utah										
Vermont									✓	meets or exceeds NADA
Virginia	✓	200 hrs							✓	
Washington	No									
West Virginia					No					
Wisconsin	✓	0		0	✓	0				
Wyoming										

TABLE 10. STATES WITHOUT ACUPUNCTURE PRACTICE ACTS

State	Acupuncture has been determined to be the practice of medicine	A non-physician acupuncturist may practice under the supervision of a licensed physician
Alabama		No
Delaware	Yes	
Kansas		Yes
Kentucky	Yes	No
Michigan	Yes	Yes
Mississippi		No
North Dakota	Yes	
Oklahoma		
South Dakota		
Wyoming		

"Yes" indicates confirmation of the information by a state agency.

"No" indicates confirmation of the information by a state agency.

A blank cell indicates that the information was undetermined or unavailable at the time this book was researched.

The information contained in this, and other tables, is subject to change at any time. The reader is advised to contact individual state boards for the most current and complete information.

ALASKA

Ms. P.J. Gingras
Division of Occupational Licensing-Acupuncture
PO Box 11086
Juneau, AK 99811-0806
(907) 465-2695
(907) 465-2974 FAX
www.commerce.state.ak.us/occ/

ARIZONA

Mr. Allen Imig
Acupuncture Board of Examiners
1400 West Washington, Suite 230
Phoenix, AZ 85007
(602) 542-3095
(602) 542-3093 FAX
www.azacuboard.az.gov

ARKANSAS

Board of Acupuncture and Related Techniques
813 West 3rd Street
Little Rock, AR 72201
(501) 683-3583
(501) 244-2333 FAX
www.asbart.org

CALIFORNIA

Ms. Marilyn Nielsen
Department of Consumer Affairs
Acupuncture Board
444 North 3rd Street, Suite 260
Sacramento, California 95814
(916) 445-3021
(916) 445-3015 Fax
www.acupuncture.ca.gov

COLORADO

Mr. Kevin Heupel
Department of Regulatory Agencies
Office of Acupuncturists Licensure
1560 Broadway, Suite 1340
Denver, CO 80202-5140
(303) 894-7429
(303) 894-7764
www.dora.state.co.us/acupuncturists

CONNECTICUT

Ms. Lawanda Scott
Department of Public Health
Acupuncture Licensing Section
PO Box 340308
Hartford, CT 06134-0308
(860) 509-8388
(860) 509-8457 FAX
www.dph.state.ct.us

DISTRICT OF COLUMBIA

Mr. Jim Granger, Jr.
Department of Health
Advisory Committee on Acupuncture
825 North Capitol Street NE, Room 2224
Washington, DC 20002
(202) 442-4777
(202) 442-9431 Fax
www.dchealth.dc.gov

FLORIDA

Ms. Ronda Bryan
Division of Medical Quality Assurance
Board of Acupuncture
4052 Bald Cypress Way
Bin #C06
Tallahassee, FL 32399
(850) 245-4586
(850)921-6184 FAX
www.doh.state.fl.us/mqa/acupuncture/
acu_home.html

GEORGIA

Ms. LaSharn Hughes
Georgia Board of Medical Examiners
2 Peachtree Street NW
Atlanta, GA 30303-3159
(404) 656-3913
(404) 656-9723 FAX
www.sos.state.ga.us/ebd-medical

HAWAII

Ms. Christine Rutkowski
Department of Commerce and Consumer Affairs
Professional and Vocational Licensing Division
Board of Acupuncture
PO Box 3469
Honolulu, HI 96801
(808) 586-3000 (application information)
FAX: not available
www.state.hi.us/dcca

IDAHO

Ms. Sandee Hitesman
Bureau of Occupational Licenses
Board of Acupuncture
1109 Main Street, Suite 220
Boise, ID 83702-5642
(208) 334-3233
(208) 334-3945 Fax
www.ibol.idaho.gov/acu.htm

ILLINOIS

Ms. Sandra Dunn
Department of Professional Regulation
320 West Washington Street, 3rd Floor
Springfield, IL 62786
(217) 782-8556
(217) 524-2169 FAX
(217) 524-6735 TDD
www.ildfpv.com

INDIANA

Ms. Angela Smith-Jones, J.D.
Health Professions Bureau
Medical Licensing Board
402 West Washington, Room 041
Indianapolis, IN 46204
(317) 234-2060
(317) 233-4236 FAX
www.state.in.us/hpb/

IOWA

Ms. Amy Van Maanen
Board of Medical Examiners
400 SW 8th Street, Suite C
Des Moines, IA 50309-4686
(515) 281-6492
(515) 242-5908 FAX
www.docboard.org/ia/acup.htm

LOUISIANA

Ms. Sandra Broussard
Board of Medical Examiners
630 Camp Street
PO Box 30250
New Orleans, LA 70112-1449
(504) 568-6820 ext 227
(504) 599-0503 FAX
www.lsbme.org

MAINE

Ms. Geraldine L. Betts, Administrator
Professional and Financial Regulation
Office of Licensing and Registration
#35 State House Station
Augusta, ME 04333
(207) 624-8600
(207) 624-8637 FAX
(207) 624-8563 TDD
www.maineprofessionalreg.org

MARYLAND

Ms. Penny Heisler
Board of Acupuncture
Room 321
4201 Patterson Avenue
Baltimore, MD 21215
(410) 764-4766 / (800) 530-2481
(410) 358-7258 FAX
www.dhmh.state.md.us/bacc

MASSACHUSETTS

Ms. Ann Marie Casey
Board of Registration in Medicine
Committee on Acupuncture
560 Harrison Avenue, Suite G4
Boston, MA 02118
(617) 654-9869
(617) 357-8453
www.massmedboard.org/acupuncture

MINNESOTA

Ms. Jeanne Hoffman
Board of Medical Practice
University Park Plaza
2829 University Avenue SE, Suite 500
Minneapolis, MN 55414-3246
(612) 617-1230
(612) 617-2166 FAX
www.bmp.state.mn.us

MISSOURI

Ms. Loree Kessler
Acupuncturist Advisory Committee
PO Box 1335
Jefferson City, MO 65102-1335
(573) 526-1555
(573) 751-0735 FAX
http://pr.mo.gov

MONTANA

Ms. Evie Martin
Department of Labor and Industry
Board of Medical Examiners
PO Box 200513
Helena, MT 59620-0513
(406) 841-2364
(406) 841-2343 FAX
www.discoveringmontana.com/dli/bsd

NEBRASKA
Ms. Vicki Bumgarner
Nebraska Health and Human Services
Credentialing Division
301 Centennial Mall South
PO Box 94986
Lincoln, NE 68509-4986
(402) 471-4911
(402) 471-3577 FAX
(402) 471-9570 TDD
www.state.ne.us

NEVADA
Ms. Amy Richards
Board of Oriental Medicine
9775 S Maryland Parkway, Suite F-280
Las Vegas, NV 89123
(702) 837-8921
(702) 914-8921 FAX
www.oriental_medicine.state.nv.us

NEW HAMPSHIRE
Ms. Ruth Walter, Licensing Clerk
Board of Acupuncture Licensing
Department of Health and Human Services
Office of Program Support
129 Pleasant Street, Brown Building
Concord, NH 03301-3857
(603) 271-0853
(603) 271-5590 FAX
www.dhhs.nh.gov

NEW JERSEY
Ms. Terri Goldberg
Division of Consumer Affairs
Board of Medical Examiners
Acupuncture Examining Board
124 Halsey Street, 6th Floor
Newark, NJ 07102
(973) 273-8092
(973) 273-8075 FAX
www.state.nj.us/lps/ca/medical.htm

NEW MEXICO
Ms. Rosemarie Ortiz
Board of Acupuncture and Oriental Medicine
PO Box 25101
Santa Fe, NM 87504
(505) 476-4630
(505) 476-4545
www.rld.state.nm.us

NEW YORK
Ms. Ronnie Hausheer
New York Board for Acupuncture
Education Building, 2W
89 Washington Avenue
Albany, NY 12234
(518) 474-3817 Ext. 100
(518) 486-4846 FAX
www.op.nysed.gov/acupun.htm

NORTH CAROLINA
Ms. Paola Ribadeneira
Acupuncture Licensing Board
PO Box 10686
Raleigh, NC 27605
(919) 821-3008
(919) 833-5743 FAX
www.ncalb.state.nc.us

OHIO
Mr. Tom Dilling, J.D., Director
Ohio State Medical Board
77 South High Street, 17th Floor
Columbus, OH 43215-6127
(614) 466-3934
(614) 728-5946 FAX
www.med.ohio.gov

OREGON
Ms. Diana Dolstra
Board of Medical Examiners
620 Crowne Plaza
1500 SW First Avenue
Portland, OR 97201-5770
(503) 229-5770
(503) 229-6543 FAX
www.bme.state.or.us

PENNSYLVANIA
Ms. Gina Bittner
Board of Medicine
Board of Osteopathic Medicine
PO Box 2649
Harrisburg, PA 17105
(717) 783-4858
(717) 783-7769 FAX
www.dos.state.pa.us

ACUPUNCTURE & ORIENTAL MEDICINE REGULATORY AGENCIES

RHODE ISLAND
Ms. Kelly Doyle
Department of Health and Professional Regulation
Cannon Building
Three Capitol Hill, Room 104
Providence, RI 02908
(401) 222-2828
(401) 222-1272 FAX
www.health.state.ri.us

SOUTH CAROLINA
Ms. Annette Disher
Department of Labor and Licensing
Board of Medical Examiners
110 Centerview Drive, Suite 202
PO Box 11289
Columbia, SC 29211-1289
(803) 896-4500
(803) 896-4515 FAX
www.llr.state.sc.us

TENNESEE
Ms. Marsha Arnold
Advisory Committee for Acupuncture
Cordell Hull Building, 1st Floor
425 Fifth Avene North
Nashville, TN 37247-1010
(615) 532-4384
(615) 253-4484 FAX
www.state.tn.us/health

TEXAS
Mr. Tim Speer
Texas State Board of Medical Examiners
PO Box 2018, MC-231
Austin, TX 78768-2018
(512) 305-7067
(512) 305-9416 FAX
www.tsbme.state.tx.us

UTAH
Mr. Daniel T. Jones, Bureau Manager
Occupational and Professional Licensing
160 East 300 South, Box 146741
Salt Lake City, UT 84114-6741
(801) 530-6767
(801) 530-6511
www.dopl.utah.gov

VERMONT
Ms. Loris Rollins, Unit Administrator
Office of Professional Regulation
26 Terrace Street, Drawer 09
Montpelier, VT 05609-1106
(802) 828-2191
(802) 828-2465 FAX
www.vtprofessionals.org

VIRGINIA
Ms. Ola Powers/Ms. Pam Nicholson
Board of Medicine
6603 West Broad Street, 5th Floor
Richmond, VA 23230-1712
(804) 662-7405
(804) 662-7281
www.dhp.virginia.gov

WASHINGTON
Ms. Vicki Brown
Department of Health
Health Professions Quality Assurance
310 Israel Road
PO Box 47860
Tumwater WA 98501-7860
(360) 236-4865
(360) 664-9077 FAX
www.dol.wa.gov/main/biglist.htm

WEST VIRGINIA
Mr. C.P. Negri, President
Board of Acupuncture
364 High Street, Suite 203
Morgantown, WV 26505
(304) 529-4558
(304) 529-3710 FAX
www.wvs.state.wv.us/acupuncture

WISCONSIN
Dr. Kimberly M. Nania, Director
Cathy Pond, Credentialing Administrator
Department of Regulation and Licensing
Bureau of Health Service Professions
Acupuncture Certification
1400 East Washington Avenue
Madison, WI 53708-8935
(608) 266-2112
(608) 267-3816 FAX
http://drl.wi.gov

NATIONAL ACUPUNCTURE & ORIENTAL MEDICINE ORGANIZATIONS

Accreditation Commission for Acupuncture and Oriental Medicine (ACAOM)
Maryland Trade Center #3
7501 Greenway Center Drive, Suite 820
Greenbelt, MD 20770
(301) 313-0855
(301) 313-0912 FAX
www.acaom.org

Acupuncture and Oriental Medicine Alliance (AOMALLIANCE)
6405 43rd Avenue CT NW, Ste B
Gig Harbor, Washington 98335
(253) 851-6896
(253) 851-6883 FAX
www.aomalliance.org

American Academy of Medical Acupuncture (AAMA)
4929 Wilshire Boulevard
Suite 428
Los Angeles, California 90010
(323) 937-5514
www.medicalacupuncture.org

American Association of Oriental Medicine (AAOM)
909 22nd Street
Sacramento, CA 95816
PO Box 162340
Sacramento, CA 95816
(916) 443-4770
(916) 443-4766 FAX
www.aaom.org

American Organization for Bodywork Therapies of Asia (AOBTA)
1010 Haddonfield-Berlin Rd Ste 408
Voorhees NJ 08043
(856)782-1616
(856)782-1653 FAX
www.aobta.org

Council of Colleges of Acupncture and Oriental Medicine (CCAOM)
3909 National Drive, Suite 125
Burtonsville, MD 20866
(301) 476-7790
(301) 476-7792 FAX
www.ccaom.org

Federation of Acupuncture and Oriental Medicine Regulatory Agencies (FAOMRA)
c/o Penny Heisler, Treasurer
Maryland Board of Acupuncture
4201 Patterson Avenue
Baltimore, MD 21215
(410)764-4766
www.faomra.com

National Acupuncture Detoxification Association (NADA)
PO Box 1927
Vancouver, WA 98668-1927
360-254-0186
360-260-8620 FAX
www.acudetox.com

National Acupuncture Foundation (NAF)
15228 Rosemary Loop SE
Olalla, WA 98359
(253) 851-6538
(253) 851-6538 FAX
www.nationalacupuncturefoundation.org

National Certification Commission for Acupuncture and Oriental Medicine (NCCAOM)
11 Canal Center Plaza, Suite 300
Alexandria, Virginia 22314
(703) 548-9004
(703) 548-9079 FAX
www.nccaom.org

Complementary and Alternative Medicine Law Blog
Law Offices of Michael H. Cohen
770 Mass. Ave.
POBox 391108
Cambridge, MA 02139
(617) 825-3368
(617) 825-9116 FAX
www.camlawblog.com

Federation of Chiropractic Licensing Boards
5401 W 10th Street, Suite 101
Greeley, CO 80634-4400
(970) 356-3500
(970) 356-3599 FAX
www.fclb.org

National Center for Complementary and Alternative Medicine
NCCAM Clearinghouse
PO Box 7923
Gaithersburg, MD 20898
(888) 644-6226 toll free
(866) 464-3616 FAX
www.nccam.nih.gov

National Chiropractic Board of Examiners
901 54th Avenue
Greeley, Colorado 80634
970-356-9100
www.ncbe.org

North American Commision of Acupuncture and Oriental Medicine (NACAOM) (formerly the NAFTA Commission)
PO Box 726
Point Reyes Station, CA 94956
www.nacaom.org

Society for Acupuncture Research
www.acupunctureresearch.org

U.S. Department of Health and Human Services
200 Independence Avenue, S.W.
Washington, D.C. 20201
(202) 619-0257
(877) 696-6775 toll free

World Health Organization
Guidelines on Basic Training and Safety in Acupuncture (document)
http://whqlibdoc.who.int/hq/1999/WHO_EDM_TRM_99.1.pdf

The purchase of this book supports the ongoing programs of
the National Acupuncture Foundation.
Please visit our web site at
www.nationalacupuncturefoundation.org
for information about the NAF.